1

Other titles by the same author

Flamenco Heritage: The Clan of El Pinini
ISBN: 13:978-1508953579

Gitanerías: The Essence of Flamenco
ISBN: 13:978-1512137590

Andalusia: Between Dream and Reality.
ISBN: 13:978-1975830489

Seville: A City of Marvels.
ISBN: 979 – 8631650091

A Cohort of Creative Bohemians
and other interesting individuals
ISBN: 9798814863751

Flamenco:

An Englishman's passion

Tony Bryant

First published in 2006 by flamenco sapiens (Seville)

Second edition published in 2011 by Sol y Sombra Books (Málaga)

Third edition published in 2024 by Jato Editorial (Seville)

ISBN: 13:978-1508418535

ISBN: 10:1508418535

To Javier, thank you.

While it is important to learn rules at the outset of one's career, an artiste must discard them, because art springs from the soul, not some pre-existing code.

Federico García Lorca

Flamenco: An Englishman's Passion

Preface to new edition

This book was first published by *flamenco sapiens* (Seville) in 2006, and to mark its coming of age, I decided to revise and re-edit it for its third edition. Although new photographs have been included, I decided not to adjust the tense of the text with reference to the flamenco artistes who have died over the last 18 years, and there have been many. These have included two of the greatest female flamenco singers of the twentieth century, La Fernanda and La Bernarda de Utrera, who died in 2006 and 2009 respectively. The funeral of La Fernanda de Utrera was one of the grandest Utrera had seen for many years and the service had an air of stateliness, which was nothing more than expected for such a revered woman. Politicians interrupted their sessions to acknowledge the passing of this celebrated singer, and television personalities, musicians and matadors remembered her with tenderness.

The funeral service of her sister, La Bernarda de Utrera, was held in the church of *Santiago el Mayor*, during which the priest described Bernarda as the complement of her sister – 'like cotton and silk' Their tomb had been donated by the local council and, even though Fernanda had died three years previous, Bernarda was the first to occupy the tomb, because it was not finished until just before Bernarda died. The family have since made the difficult decision to have

Fernanda's body disentombed and placed in the new shrine so that the sisters can rest together for eternity.

Chano Lobato, considered the greatest living interpreter of the cantes de Cádiz, died at the age of 82 in his home in Seville in April 2009. Chano had been in a delicate state of health for some time and his appearances on the flamenco scene were limited in the last year of his life. As he once claimed while talking about his failing health, 'If I was removed from the stage I would surely die'.

Enrique Morente died in 2010, and a lawsuit was issued by his family, who declared that his death was caused by negligence. Morente, since called the 'Pope of Flamenco', died in a Madrid hospital after an alleged surgical error during a relatively straightforward stomach operation.

One of the biggest shocks came in 2014, when Paco de Lucía suffered a fatal heart attack on a beach in Mexico while on holiday with his family. Paco's family summed up the tragic news up with a statement: 'There is no solace for those who knew and loved him, or for the thousands of his fans that did not know him personally. For this reason, we want to share with you all a hug and a tear, but also the conviction that Paco lived as he wanted and died playing with his children by the sea'. 'His life provided us with some wonderful years and he filled this world with beauty.'

Paco's body was repatriated the following day and his coffin, draped with the Spanish flag, was taken to Madrid and laid in the National

Auditorium of Music: thousands of fans queued for up to five hours in order to pay their respects, before his body was transported to his birth place, and to his final resting place. The coffin, draped with the flags of Spain and Andalusia, was met with a ten-minute ovation, but his family had wanted a quiet funeral and so only family and very close friends witnessed the interment - one of who was Camarón de la Isla's widow, La Chispa.

El Lebrijano died at his home in Seville just a few days after leaving hospital following surgery on a previously undetected heart problem in 2016. Following his death, Lebrija town hall declared three days of mourning. El Lebrijano's coffin, draped with the Gypsy flag, and those of Andalusia and Lebrija, was laid in the Juan Bernabe theatre so people could pay their last respects.

Other losses included guitarist Moraito Chico, who died after a relatively short battle with cancer in 2011; Chiquito de la Calzada in 2012, one of Malaga's most popular singers who went on to enjoy a successful career as a comedian; and Curro de Utrera, one of Utrera's greatest singers of fandangos, in 2015.

But it has not been all bad news, because today flamenco seems to be gaining much world-wide recognition and it appears that, even though the commercial scene is by far the most preferred, there are many new flamenco aficionados who crave the more orthodox styles of this art.

I hope that this new version of *Flamenco: An Englishman's Passion* will help the reader to understand and appreciate the art of flamenco.

My basic views and fundamental beliefs have not changed following years of maturing within the art of flamenco, if anything, they are now even more strongly implanted with time and experience.

Foreword

Flamenco is a hard church.

Of all the minority musical forms it is the one where even the most casual aficionado needs a certain level of familiarity to enjoy it. It is not easy listening and without the most basic awareness of styles and rhythm, is meaningless.

On the plus side, it has to be admitted that many musical forms that are the preserve of racial minorities are almost impenetrable to people not belonging to that minority, mainly due to the desire for the music to be kept exclusive to the minority in question.

The Romany music of Eastern Europe for example is a zealously-guarded area where outsiders are not welcome, and often actively discouraged. But since the emphasis is on instrumental adroitness it is hard to see why a non-Romany should be considered as a less talented player than a Gypsy. It must be a purely business-related consideration.

Spanish flamenco is rather different. In spite of what is commonly believed - that the dance is the pivotal endeavour, as some readers of this book will discover, flamenco can and does thrive without dancers, and indeed even without guitarists. In some modest get-togethers there is no guitar available and the singer will be accompanied by nothing more than rhythmic hand-clapping or discreet table-tapping.

Tony Bryant makes this point well, and also leads the reader elegantly from what is generally known as commercial flamenco to authentic *cante jondo*, with stops in between. And he has been fortunate, as indeed I have, because Spanish Gypsies that live from flamenco do not try to dominate the art, having realised that non-Gypsies can perform as well as Gypsies, certainly in the vocal department. As Tony documents flawlessly, there have been many great singers who did not possess the *voz afillá*, the gravelly hoarse voice of the true Gypsy *cantaor*. And non-Gypsy guitarists and dancers are common.

All this may make it easier for a non-Gypsy Spaniard to enter the fray, but what about an unusually tall Englishman with a limited knowledge of the language? The book contains some very honest and self-deprecating accounts of Tony's occasionally fraught attempts to get through the small door that leads to the garden where he wanted to be. Full marks for not being afraid to be laughed at, but the overriding question is why?

As an ex-drummer in an English rock band, Tony was initially baffled by flamenco rhythms (nothing new here; every newcomer is), and try as he might could find no connection with the world of rhythm and blues. As he astutely points out, Western music uses only the major and minor scales, while flamenco also uses the Phrygian mode (*modo dórico* in Spanish). Indeed, thesis have been written about the flamenco beat, and there is nothing more absurd (or in bad taste) than a spectator at a flamenco party trying ineffectually to mark time. The twelve-beat cycle is unique to the art form.

There have been other books by foreigners, usually Anglo-Saxons, who attempted to enter the flamenco world with various degrees of success. The American, Donn Pohren, was the first with his ground-breaking works, The Art of Flamenco (1962) and Lives and Legends of Flamenco (1964); Gerald Howson, a proficient guitarist wrote the classic Flamencos of Cádiz Bay in 1965; and Duende by Jason Webster has been a much more recent success on a predominantly similar theme.

Tony's book is different – mainly because he has been an intelligent spectator with a gift for drilling down into the history of this great art with a perception and an enthusiasm bordering on the academic – and possessing a sense of humour that sets him apart. He strives for nothing more than the fulfilment of a burning desire to learn as much about flamenco as any human being on the planet, and I doubt very much that this will be his last book on the subject.

Andrew J Linn

Books4Spain. Málaga

Acknowledgments

It was very hard to put into writing the names of all the people who have helped me with this book, because many of them did so without even realising that they had. They are not in any way listed in order of how precious their contribution was, because all of the help I received was monumental.

One person to who I am greatly indebted is Javier Martinez Jiménez. Javier has acted as my translator and interpreter, and I also need to thank him for the many hours of discussion (sometimes heated, especially where the art of the *corrida* was concerned) and for his information on Seville, *Semana Santa*, and the *Sevillanas*.

To El Museo del Baile Flamenco, especially Dr Kurt Grötsch, I would like to extend my extreme gratitude for his continued confidence.

To my very good friend María, in whose house it all started, and has since continued. Some of my most memorable nights were spent sat around the *mesa camilla* in her house talking until the early hours, or at least until the wine ran out. A mesa camilla is a wonderful invention, although not the sort of thing you would expect to find in the hot Andalusian capital. During the winter months Seville is extremely cold, and one will find that most houses possess one of these essential luxuries. It is always the central point of the house during the winter and I have the fondest memories of listening to many a tale while huddled under the heavy blanket-tablecloth to keep warm.

To Hugo, who has constantly been at my side in Seville and Málaga, keeping me sane when all else failed.

To simply say thank you to José Losada - El Carrete - would be an injustice, because he has shown me so much warmth and understanding on the many occasions when I have sought his knowledge. It is the characters such as El Carrete that make flamenco what it is today.

I would like to extend a sincere thank you to Lucía Miralles, whose help and introductions were incalculable.

Finally, I need to thank all the people whose lives I have interrupted while compiling this book, whether it be only to ask for directions to a *peña,* or just to talk about this wonderful art.

Flamenco is about ordinary, everyday people who perform on the spur of the moment, be it at a party, a get-together, or simply because they are in the mood. For aficionados, flamenco is merely part of everyday life: for me, it has become like a cuckoo, pushing to one side all the things that were once important to me, and becoming the most fascinating phenomenon that I have ever experienced.

On many occasions, a quiet drink in a small backstreet bodega, or a birthday celebration, has erupted into an orgy of song and dance, and on these occasions, I have experienced some of the most authentic and traditional flamenco possible. The majority of these people are not professional artists; they are people who are simply enjoying life, and this enjoyment can be sparked by the simplest of things.

Introduction

Al Andaluz is the name that the invading Muslims christened a mysterious paradise located in the Southern-most part of Spain. Andalusia's Arabic past is evident and recalls the near 800 years that the Moors ruled here. In Seville, there is the magnificent *Giralda* tower, built between 1172-1195; in Granada, the breathtaking *Alhambra Palace*; and the colossal *Mezquita* in Córdoba, the Muslim capital of Al Andaluz.

Andalusia is full of life, colour, romance, music and dancing, of plucked guitar strings, the snapping of fingers and clicking castanets, of happiness and sorrow, of artistes, poets and writers - but most of all it is a land of passion, culture and history.

It is a hard and dusty mountainous landscape, where men dressed in gold-trimmed suits do battle with massive bulls in a ring that echoes the shouts of Roman gladiators.

It is a land of wine and sherry, of olive groves, and of fruit trees, their burdens ripening in the burning sun.

Andalusia is a land where strange ritual celebrations occur during Easter week, when scenes of the Passion are paraded through the streets, trumpets blaring, drums pounding and cymbals crashing, while people cast themselves before the floats, sobbing uncontrollably.

It is a land of *fiestas* and celebrations, where one week of the year every town holds its *feria*, a week of dressing up in traditional costume to parade through the streets during daylight and party at the fair into the dark hours.

Andalusia is the place that, in the early 15th century, a race of people called the *Zincali* made their home. They were met with mixed feelings of fascination, mystery, revulsion, and fear. *Cali* is their language and *calo* is the name by which they refer to themselves. In Spanish they are known as *gitanos* - Gypsies.

This book focuses on my passionate love of music. Perhaps it might answer the oft-asked question of how an Englishman can hold such a burning passion for a culture so different to his own.

I have no idea how it came to be so intense; I only know that to discover something that can make one feel as I feel, something that has touched my life and my soul in such a mystical way, is a precious gift.

Unclean music

I was born in Stockwell, South London, in 1961 - a time when the UK was beginning to dominate the world music scene. Four Liverpudlians from working-class backgrounds were about to change the face of modern music. Even today, more than sixty years after The Beatles first conquered the world, the phenomenon is still going strong, even though many of their younger fans were not even conceived when the group separated in 1970.

Thirty-five years previous, the Nazis had banned jazz music as it was considered the curse of the Jews and Negroes, an unclean music that was to be eliminated in the interests of cultural purity. All music recorded by non-Aryan artistes was banned in Germany in 1938, but things were a little more lenient in Nazi-occupied Europe during WWII.

In Paris, for example, musicians like the jazz guitarist Django Reinhardt were relatively free to promote their music, even though Django was of Gypsy blood, a race that was also persecuted by the Nazis during the occupation.

Prior to the 1950s, music in countries like Spain was behind the rest of Europe. General Francisco Franco had had a tight grip on the country since his victory in the Spanish Civil War in 1939, and many of Spain's top musicians and artists fled their homeland in preference of Latin American countries.

The people of Andalusia were shut off from the outside world, and, in fact, Andalusia was shut off from the rest of Spain. Franco had deserted this region and left it to rot, and the people of Andalusia had to fend for themselves. For this reason, flamenco was not influenced by other world music, other than its opera period when classical music inspired the dance and song, but not to the extent that world music has since influenced flamenco.

Spain's doors remained tightly shut to the outside world and it was not until Franco died in 1975 that the youth of Spain experienced an exciting new wave of music, which England and America had dominated since the '60s. Rock and roll started the new teenage movement towards rebellion against parents everywhere from America to England.

Rhythm and blues, an umbrella term given to what was originally called 'race music', was a name invented by the American Billboard magazine used to describe any music that was sung or written by black Americans. This music was to receive much criticism, and artistes like Ray Charles were attacked for mixing the blues with spirituals and gospel music. Even Elvis was criticised by people angered that a white rock and roll artiste should mix his music with gospel.

Jazz artistes also began fusing jazz with different styles of music, especially trumpeter Miles Davis, who was at the head of this move.

In America, many of the jazz greats like Lester Young, Stan Getz, and Charlie Parker were taking their music worldwide. But this was not a particularly good time for jazz musicians: those who survived the heroine epidemic were faced with racism at its worst. One needs to remember the terrible atrocities caused by America's race policies: performers like Billie Holiday and Louis Armstrong were forbidden from riding in the same elevators as the white guests at the venues where they performed.

While many of the clubs and venues hired black musicians, they kept a strict 'whites-only' policy for their customers. It wasn't until a shoe salesman by the name of Barney Josephson opened the *Café Society* in Greenwich Village in 1938 that things started to change. He opened his jazz club with the policy of whoever wanted to come and listen to the music would be allowed entry. There was to be no segregation, discrimination or racialism of the audience. It is perhaps ironic that there was never any racial tension or prejudices between the musicians that played together during the golden age of jazz.

Jazz music evolved from the slave trade in America, and the heart and soul of this music is the result of the terrible atrocities these people suffered. As a child, I had no idea about the political and social problems of the world, and my concentration stayed on the music, not the racial tensions.

I started to play the drums from an early age: my first drum was made from an old banjo which was converted into a snare drum by my uncle when I was just ten years old.

As a youngster, I had practised my drums along to the sounds of the big band jazz records of Buddy Rich and Gene Krupa.

As the roaring '60s came to an end and The Beatles were no more, the 1970s and '80s were, in my opinion, the last great era in British music. The Rolling Stones were still going strong (as they are today), and artistes like Janis Joplin and Jimmy Hendrix had teased us with just a little of their genius before self-combusting due to heavy drug abuse.

Rock music had firmly established itself on the world music scene, as open-air festivals like the Isle of Wight Festival in 1970, which attracted 600,000 people, will demonstrate.

Reggae was also taking a strong hold on the British music scene, especially in 1977, when Bob Marley arrived in London after an assassination attempt in Jamaica. It was around this time that punk and new wave arrived also, further changing the face of modern music.

I played drums with numerous bands throughout the '80s, and also made a few records, although these were not to make me my fortune.

During the late 1970s and early '80s - the punk and new wave eras - just about all of my friends were in a band; and most pubs in town centres presented live music of some sort during the weekends. Many of these pub bands were knocking out the same old songs, but at least it was live music where people would get up and play their instruments. Soon, however, the live music started to fade and the entertainment in the towns' pubs was replaced by video jukeboxes and karaoke machines.

But by the 1990s, something very different was happening on the music scene in England. Suddenly the music seemed unimportant and the charts were dominated by pretty boy-bands and annoying girlie groups who were not musicians. These groups were put together by music moguls who realised that a good-looking bunch of kids who could dance and shake their bits at the screaming teenagers would generate big bucks. Many of these groups could not play an instrument, so their concerts were performed by an ensemble of session musicians who were kept in the background so that the focus would stay on the four or five sexy lads or ladettes cavorting around the stage.

For the first time in my life, the music scene in England no longer interested me. If I went to see a live band, then that is what I expected to see.

Something touched me deep inside

In 1994, I hung up my drumsticks and moved to Málaga in southern Spain: it was here that I became obsessed with a musical style that was so different to the music I had grown up with.

I am afraid that my first impression of Spanish music was little better than what I had left behind in England. The Spanish charts were dominated by europop-style music, along with cancion Española, performed by the likes of Rocío Jurado, a kind of Spanish Shriley Bassey.

Music suddenly seemed unimportant, but I soon fell in love with Andalusia, as I had never come into contact with such a beautiful and mystifying place. I started to learn about the history of Andalusia and its cultural luminaries. Pablo Ruiz Picasso was my first taste of Spanish art, although to this day I am still not sure if I appreciate his work. I think his bohemian lifestyle appealed to me more than his art.

I was also fascinated by the life of the poet and playwright, Federico García Lorca; and even more thrilled by the image portrayed of Andalusia by the hordes of romantic writers who passed through in the 19th century.

I well remember my first visit to Seville. It took my breath away with its sheer historic beauty. Triana and the old parts of the city, like the district of La Macarena, were some of the most romantic places I had ever seen. To this day, every time I visit Seville, I feel like a different person, especially when wandering around the delightful winding streets of the old Jewish quarter.

The atmosphere in this ancient Andalusian wonder is, at times, very sleepy and subdued, but Seville is not all cobbled back streets and tranquillity.

There are the Semana Santa celebrations, which are the biggest and most dramatic events in Spain. Even after you've worn yourself out enduring a week of little or no sleep, watching the theatrical scenes of the Passion, there are just two weeks to recover before the start of the April fair.

The feria is yet another week of steady physical abuse, whether from a steady flow of *manzanilla* wine and too much *paella* and *churros*, or from the fact that Seville never sleeps during this onslaught of constant partying. Days are spent eating, drinking and making merry, and the nights raving at the fair, delving into the many *casetas,* which play host to different styles of music, especially the sevillanas.

Another aspect of Andalusian life that I became interested in was the Gypsies, or 'gitanos'. There is no explanation why this was, but these people and their culture fascinated me. I wondered why the Spanish despised them so much, and why so many laws were passed between the 15th and 18th centuries forbidding them their way of life, their identity, their dress, and their music.

King Philip II said, 'The Gypsies are not a race, but a collection of vicious people drawn from the dregs of Spanish society.'

Miguel de Cervantes wrote, 'They were brought into this world for the sole purpose of being thieves.'

However, the thing that truly captivated me was the music that these 'thieves' and 'dregs' performed. My first experience with this wonderful part of Gypsy culture was in Seville while in the house of Spanish friends. It was close to Christmas, and the drink was flowing and the conversation was becoming less understandable. To hide my embarrassment at not being able to join in the conversation, I pretended to be interested in what was on the television. My eyes were fixed, but I had no idea what I was witnessing. But slowly my boredom turned into a genuine interest at what was happening on the television.

There were two performers, one on the guitar, the other singing (if one could refer to it as such). They were performing in a manner I had never seen in all my years as a musician. I remember thinking that the singer's face looked as though it was going to burst - red with rage, hands outstretched, but all with so much emotion and drive.

I remember being rather confused at this raw, energetic music, and looked towards María, who was born in the small village of Arahal, for an explanation. She informed me that the singer was a Gypsy called

José Mercé, and that the style of music was *cante jondo* (deep song), the purest style of orthodox flamenco.

A few months later, back in Málaga, I came across a CD by José Mercé and decided to buy it: The CD was *Aire*, which was to be the first major breakthrough in José Mercé's commercial career.

The CD contained *bulerías*, *alegrías* and *tangos*, names that meant little to me at that time. I remember being intrigued by the *martinete*, an old unaccompanied style, which sounded so un-tuneful it reminded me of nothing I had ever heard. Then there was a *rumba* complete with trumpet and percussion, and a heavy blues style number with José Mercé's course gravel voice as accompaniment. The styles of music on this disc were so varied I wondered how it could all be classed as flamenco. I later realised that the term 'flamenco' was similar to 'rhythm and blues', a term which covers a wide variety of different music that all have something in common, albeit precious little.

Some weeks later, while discussing this music with some Spanish friends, I was asked if I might like to go and see some live flamenco in a *tablao,* a flamenco club. We travelled the short journey from Torremolinos to Montemar, where we stopped outside the *Tablao el Tano*, an old establishment that sadly no longer exists.

I was a little nervous as we entered this small, dimly lit place, because it seemed as though we were entering somewhere we shouldn't. There were no windows in the dark cellar bar, and from across the room came a plump Gypsy woman who greeted us with a warm smile. In a low voice she informed us that the first drink would cost 2,000 *pesetas*, because, as she was quick to point out, there was no entrance fee. The price for each subsequent drink was reduced, but not by much.

Once I had had my first drink and managed to relax a little, I realised what an excellent atmosphere the place had, very warm and inviting, but also still very mysterious. The artistes were in conversation around the bar and, other than our party of four, the place was empty.

The owner of the club was El Tano, who was, in his day, an excellent dancer, so I was informed. He spent much of the night propped against the bar watching and encouraging the artistes as they performed.

I was excited by the music, but I could not say that I truly enjoyed or appreciated it. Although I did not understand the music, I felt attracted to it, as if it was somehow seducing me. Flamenco has so many parallels with the blues, and maybe it was this that made it all so interesting to me in the beginning.

I had so many questions, because this was so new to me, so exciting, so passionate. I felt like I had stumbled on some sort of treasure chest, not knowing what was inside, but bursting with excitement about what I had discovered.

Someone who has been fundamental in the writing of this book once said, 'You like flamenco music, but you don't live the flamenco life. It is a way of life, and the only way to truly understand this culture is by integrating into the Andalusian Gypsy flamenco community.' This is not as daunting as one might think, because these Gypsies have themselves integrated into the lifestyle of the communities in which they live more than any other Romany people.

So that is exactly what I set out to do. I knew there was more to flamenco than the music itself, and so I went in search of the mysteries of flamenco. I spent much time wandering around tiny villages that were so far off the beaten track that I felt quite alien. Even though I had begun to acquire an understanding of the Spanish language, my English accent made it obvious that I was a foreigner. For me, it was like a magical mystery tour, because I had come into contact with something that was to change my life. It can only be described as a passion, something that had gripped me deep inside and touched my soul, and to this day I have not been released, nor do I want to be.

I have come into contact with many different forms of music over the years and I always believed that no music could replace the passion I had experienced with blues and rock and roll. Jazz has played a large part in my musical education, as has reggae and folk music. In hindsight, I believe that my fascination for flamenco was instigated by my constant interest in cult music, or dare I say, music of outcast people. Whether this be the razzmatazz style music of the Gypsies, the field hollers of the African slaves, or simple redemption songs of the oppressed, music has always been my first love, but flamenco has touched me more than any other style I have been acquainted with.

Thanks to this art we call flamenco, I am a much wiser person than when I first arrived on the shores of southern Spain. Andalusia has become my home and I could not contemplate the thought of living anywhere else. I am English by birth and that can never change, but Andalusia is where my heart is.

Most of this book recounts personal experiences and tastes. My views about certain artistes and styles are a reflection of what I like and enjoy. As with any musical genre, other enthusiasts must discover their own tastes and decide for themselves who they think is best at a certain style. I only hope you have as much pleasure and satisfaction as I have had in your own quest to discover this mysterious art called flamenco.

A brief history

What is flamenco? From where and when did it evolve?

Flamenco is a passionate and seductive art form - a mysterious and misunderstood culture that has been brewing in Andalusia for approximately five centuries, and shrouded in darkness and secrecy for nearly as many. It has only in recent years become known to, but not fully understood by, the rest of the world.

Unfortunately, flamenco history has been badly documented and much of what we know comes from anecdotes and tales that have been passed down through family dynasties that have preserved these legends in much the same way as they have preserved flamenco itself.

Many different races have settled in Andalusia, all leaving their influence here. Andalusia was under the rule of the Moors for nearly 800 years, and in this time, they were said to have been hospitable, or at least tolerant, to other races, such as the Christians and Jews.

It was believed until recently that the Gypsies were the main creators of flamenco, but, although they seem to be the best and most genuine performers of it, they were not its sole creators.

The cante jondo is the coarser styles of song, and it is with these styles that the Gypsies seem to be masters. The *cante chico* refers to the small song and tends to be a lighter, more joyful styles like alegrías and the tangos.

There are also the 'cantes de ida y vuelta', which include the guajira, milonga, colombiana and the rumba. These songs are palpable evidence of how musical traditions have been intertwined through the centuries, especially during the period of colonisation and trade between Spain and the Americas.

The cante jondo is best performed with a rough, gravelly voice known as *voz afillá*, so called after the Gypsy singer, Diego el Fillo. His voice was described as burnt, cracked and dry like the Andalusian terrain.

Most people who are not familiar with this art will not realise that there is a connection between the glossy, over rehearsed, shows that are staged for the tourists, and the ancient deep styles of song and dance that have been preserved by the Gypsies of Andalusia.

But how did this great divide in flamenco come about? How is it that today we have two completely different forms of music and dance that come under the same heading of 'Flamenco'?

Orthodox flamenco differs from all other styles of world music in that even though its spontaneity and emotional depth has similarities with jazz and blues, the naturalness of the dancer and the way the singer interprets the words will ensure that no two performances can be the same.

Flamenco consists of four elements, *cante* (voice), *baile* (dance), *toque* (guitar), and the *jaleo,* which roughly translated means 'hell-raising', and involves hand-clapping, foot-stomping and shouts of encouragement. The hand-clapping or *palmas* is an art in itself and although it may look easy, it is not, as many of us have found out while trying to join in.

Duende is another important and essential part of flamenco, and some performers seem to possess this mythical power, but the duende is shrouded in as much mystery as flamenco itself. Writers and poets have given duende an almost supernatural meaning, a kind of intangible significance that goes beyond normal perception.

One aspect we can be sure of is that in its most pure and original form flamenco was only voice, a primitive cry or chant accompanied only by rhythm that would be beaten out with a cane or by the singer's bare knuckles. These styles are known as *a palo seco*, unaccompanied styles, which include the *toñas*, deblas, and martinetes - the oldest forms of flamenco song known today. Some academics have claimed that the debla was part of a religious Gypsy rite, although there is no evidence to support this.

These deep songs were initially without musical accompaniment. The addition of the guitar is surrounded in apparent mystery because the exact period that it was introduced as an accompanying instrument for flamenco is not known.

These songs were sung about suffering, persecution, hunger, lost love and death, and they include upwards of fifty different palos.

The *carceleras* are the prison songs; probably sung by the Gypsies who had been imprisoned during their persecution in Spain. *Carcel* means prison.

The martinete is the song of the blacksmiths. When the Gypsies were forced to give up their wandering lifestyles by Queen Isabella in 1499, many took to the forges for work. Their unhappiness at not being able to live their nomadic life styles was poured out in song, the hammers they worked with beating out the rhythm. The martinete derives from the word *martilla,* for hammer, being the oldest flamenco songs and probably the hardest to appreciate.

The *toñas,* the group to which all the above belong, are the hardest form on the ear for the uninitiated.

The *caracole* is associated with Madrid, and the snail-sellers who had their stalls in the streets of the capital. This group includes the *romeras* and the *mirabrás.*

The *petenera* is a very sad and haunting song style: the singer Pastora Pavón - Niña de los Peines - (girl of the combs), is said to have performed it with brilliance. The legend behind La Petenera is that she was a girl from Paterna, in Cádiz, who had a reputation for being a destroyer of men's hearts, teasing and notoriously flirting with all men.

One day she was brutally murdered by one of her spurned lovers: this story is the theme around which the lyrics are normally woven.

The *siguiriya,* which is at the heart of cante jondo, is indisputably Gypsy. It is believed to have originated in Jerez de la Frontera, although Seville is another area to which it is linked. It normally sings of sorrow, heartbreak and persecution.

Among outstanding singers of the siguiriyas was the Sevillian, Manolo Caracol, who was said to have been able to reduce grown men to tears with his duende.

The *soleares* family includes the *soleá*, of which one singer by the name of La Fernanda de Utrera was, in many aficionado's minds, the undisputed queen. This family also includes the *polo* and *caña,* which are thought to originate from Málaga, and the *alboreá*, which is the Gypsy wedding song.

The alboreá is sung and danced to the bride and groom after the bride has been proven a virgin. It is the *mataora* who carries out the test of a bride's innocence. Traditionally, she inserts a white handkerchief into the bride's vagina and, when she removes it, there will be spots of blood on it if the bride is a virgin. The handkerchief is then displayed to the families and the guests, and the festivities can begin. If, however, there were any *gachos* or non-Gypsies at the wedding (which would have been very rare), they would be asked to leave whilst the alboreá was performed, as it was believed to be unlucky for it to be heard by anyone other than a Gypsy.

The *cantiñas,* the group that includes the alegría, are the festive songs from Cádiz and, as one would expect, are lively and happy. They originated in Galicia and the name derives from the verb cantiñear, which means improvised or spontaneous song.

The gypsies put them to the rhythm of the alegría and as they began to reach Jerez de la Frontera and the surrounding towns of Seville, they developed into the style that would eventually become the bulería. The cantiñas were the most popular style of festive songs before the bulería took over in the late nineteenth century, although they were not called bulerías. These songs, regardless of the names they were given (such as jaleos), fell into the category of the modern bulería, a style full of powerful rhythms and riotous jaleo.

The *tango* is another Gypsy song style, not to be confused with the Argentinean dance. This group also includes the *tientos, tientos-tangos* and *tanguillos.*

So, flamenco is not one form of music, but a name that refers to a family of *palos* (song styles), of which there are upwards of fifty.

During the 19th century, there were, of course, no recording facilities, so singers would walk from village to village to listen to other singers in order to learn the variations of styles that evolved in different areas. The singers had to rely on memory and sometimes, during the long journey back to their hometowns and villages, the memory faded. It was interesting to hear what the singer, Fosforito, had to say about learning the styles. 'People did not use records to learn the styles, but learned at fiestas, weddings and baptisms. Whole families would attend and, after the celebrations, everyone would go home, taking with them a series of imprecise memories, and it's exactly that imprecision that opens up its own creativity. If your memory of a voice or song is vivid, you begin to reshape the sound, hence something new will emerge.'

George Borrow, a writer and bible seller in Spain during the 19th century, is often looked upon as a source of trustworthy information on the origins and music of the Gypsies. Borrow was the author of *The Zincali: An Account of the Gypsies of Spain.* This book is an in-depth look into the world of the Spanish Gypsies and is highly recommended for those interested in learning about the Gypsy culture. He spent many years observing the Gypsies, their music and dance, the myths and the legends, and for these reasons, his work is often used in the research of the origins of flamenco.

During his stay in Andalusia, George Borrow gained the trust of the Gypsies and was welcomed into Gypsy life, even to the extent of learning their language. It is a brutally honest and often shocking account of their lifestyles, customs and music. Some of today's theories concerning the early days of this art have been based on Borrow's writings. He is often quoted with reference to the origins of flamenco song, because he was experiencing this music before it had the label of flamenco attached to it.

He gives this account of the flamenco song: 'The musician composes it at the stretch of his voice, whilst his fingers are tugging at the guitar; which style of composition is by no means favourable to a long and connected series of thought. Of course, the greater part of this species of poetry perishes as soon as born. A stanza, however, is sometimes caught up by the bystander, and committed to memory and, being frequently repeated, makes in time the circuit of the country.'

He also noted that many of the songs that he heard around 1830 were written down as soon as they were created and that they normally originated 'in the midst of a circle of these singular people, dancing and singing to their wild music.'

When the Gypsies arrived in Andalusia in 1425, they brought with them many song and dance styles that had strong Indian connections.

Once the re-conquest of Andalusia was complete in 1492, the Catholic Monarchs (Isabella I and Ferdinand II) issued many decrees against the Moors, the Jews and, eventually, the Gypsies. They were driven out of Spain, or forced into hiding. Those that remained lived on the fringes of society virtually unheard of to the outside world. Bands of Gypsies and other races outcast by the *Inquisition* took refuge in the treacherous mountain terrain and areas that were too desolate for the authorities to pursue them. Three hundred years later, after the laws had been relaxed, these outcasts descended from the mountains bringing with them an exciting, colourful and seductive fusion of music and dance. This melting pot of cultures is what many theorists believe to be the prototype of flamenco, a mixture of Arabic, Gypsy and Jewish music.

There is also a fanciful theory that this mix of cultures is the blend that makes up the Andalusian Gypsies, as it is believed by some theorists that they are of a different branch to the Romany Gypsies.

The name flamenco was not used until approximately 1837. Theories abound about the origins of the name, but even today, those origins remain shrouded in folklore, so no one can be certain how the name came about. One theory is that it was taken from the Arabian word *fellah mengu*, which roughly translates as fugitive peasant. Another theory, although a little fanciful, is that flamenco referred to the Gypsy men with their underfed, spindly legs wrapped in tight trousers, and their flamboyant dress, which likened them to a flamingo.

One interesting hypothesis, which is probably more accurate, is based on the work of George Borrow. He said that the Gypsies were referred to as Flemings or Germans.

Borrow claims that after the expulsion of the Moors and the Jews, parts of Andalusia were left almost uninhabited and without skilled labourers, and this prompted King Carlos III to seek the help of a Bavarian adventurer by the name of Colonel Thurriegel. He asked the colonel to supply six thousand sturdy labourers from Flanders and

Germany. They were each to be given a smallholding, cattle, sheep, even financial help; their part being to harvest the land and take up the occupations vacated by the departing Moors and Jews.

What the colonel delivered, according to Borrow, was a rabble of six thousand vagabonds and wanderers. These people quickly tired of their new settled life style and soon returned to their wandering, stealing and begging. To the Andalusian people, especially the farmers and landowners, who were very often the victims of these itinerant bands, they became known as Germans and Flemings.

By 1830, the term German had been dropped, and the name Fleming (flamenco) was used to describe these wanderers. Some years later, the term flamenco was also applied to the music that these people performed. At first, it was not considered worthy of attention, as it was only performed in the close-knit communities and private get-togethers of the Gypsies.

What is known about the early flamenco singers comes from the first writers on the subject. Antonio Machado y Alvarez (Demófilo), who was the father of the playwrights, Manuel and Antonio Machado, was thought to be one of the first *flamencologists*.

Another writer on the subject was Serafín Estébanez Calderón - El Solitario, who was born in Málaga in 1799. Although from Málaga, Calderón's work was most often based on his experiences in Seville. This included Un Baile en Triana, from his most famous work, Escenas

Andaluzas (Andalusian tales). In this, he describes a Gypsy fiesta in Triana which was attended by one of the first documented singers, El Planeta. However, the singer and flamencologist, Antonio Mairena, believed that the Gypsies had misled Calderón, thus dismissing the accuracy of his work. Be that as it may, it was said that no one else had the ability to invoke the ambience of the taverns of Triana or that of the Gypsy culture.

Some of the earliest known singers are Tio Luis el de la Juliana, born in Jerez de la Frontera in 1760; El Planeta, most probably born in Puerto Real sometime towards the end of the 18th century; and Diego El Fillo, who was born in Cádiz in 1800.

Francisco Ortega Vargas, El Fillo is remembered for his siguiriyas, especially the siguiriya describing the murder of his brother, Juan Encueros, who was stabbed to death in a street fight.

These first noted flamenco performers were to pass the secret of their art on to the next generation of singers, such as Tomás el Nitri, and El Loco Mateo, who was considered one of the greatest singers of the soleá.

Tomás el Nitri was born in 1830 and he secured his name in flamenco's badly documented history by becoming the first singer to be awarded the coveted *Llave de Oro del Cante*. The golden key of flamenco singing has only ever been awarded to five singers. Tomás el Nitri is reported to have received his key in the bar El Sin Techo in Málaga in

1862. However, the only proof of his award is an old sepia photograph, which shows El Nitri holding his coveted key. Some people claim that this key was actually awarded to El Nitri in Jerez de la Frontera: others dispute the authenticity of this key, claiming it is merely a photograph of the singer holding a key. The truth will never be known.

The flamenco scene started to change towards the middle of the 19th century, a time when the old Gypsy singers were becoming less popular. By the end of the century, flamenco was frowned upon by writers, politicians and the media, a trend instigated by a group of intellectuals known as the *Generation of '98*. It was of general opinion that the jondo flamenco was worthless music performed by a bunch of riff-raff, and this opened the door for a new trend in flamenco, suddenly creating a great divide.

Flamenco was about to make a move in a different direction and a more commercial style of song was to take Andalusia by storm.

One man, considered to be one of the most important singers in the history of flamenco, stood firm against this move towards the lighter styles. Born in Morón de la Frontera, Seville, in 1829, Silverio Franconetti was an Italian-descended non-Gypsy. He studied the song styles of the Gypsy masters and soon became one of the most prolific singers of flamenco song, much to the amazement of the Gypsies.

Franconetti was said to have had a voice like 'sweet honey', and that he was able to sing every style of flamenco perfectly. He opened the first café cantante - *Silverios,* a music café in Seville where artistes were hired to perform for a paying public.

It was also around this time that another non-Gypsy artiste came forward with a new style of flamenco song that was mellower than the harsh cries of the Gypsy flamenco. The *fandangos.*

Juan Breva, a singer from Veléz Málaga, performed a style known as the *malagueña.* This style of fandango evolved from the *verdiales*, a folk song performed in the mountain villages that surround Málaga. The fandangos swept across Andalusia gaining numerous interpreters that appealed to the masses, and soon café cantantes began to spring up in most cities in Andalusia in order to accommodate this new craze. One of the most famous was the Café de Chinitas in Málaga.

The café cantante period, 1850-1910, was known as the 'Golden Age', and this was the period when cante jondo started its decline, as did Silverio Franconetti.

The performers of orthodox flamenco were no longer in demand, and they were faced with the option of forsaking their art and joining the hordes of fandango style singers, or returning to their villages to continue their art virtually unnoticed by the outside world, just as it had been before.

Flamenco troupes were created, and the dance became choreographed; while a new aspect of flamenco appeared for the first time, the advent of the solo flamenco guitarist. Flamenco had become a cabaret style of entertainment and gone was all the spontaneity and character of the Gypsy song.

A few of the café cantantes survived into the 1920s, but by then flamenco had changed from its original structure, and the next few years saw a decline in the Gypsy flamenco in preference to a mindless distortion of the art.

In 1922, Spanish poet Federico García Lorca and composer Manuel de Falla, along with a collection of other writers and aficionados, decided that it was time to try to stop the cante jondo sliding into oblivion.

They invited unknown singers from all corners of Andalusia to perform in a flamenco competition that was organised to re-instate cante jondo to its rightful place. Manuel de Falla stated that interest would only be shown to those singers of the jondo songs. He also said that cante jondo was not to be confused with the commercial styles, which he referred to as 'flamenco'.

The Concurso de Cante Jondo was held in the gardens of the Alhambra Palace in Granada on the 13th and 14th of June 1922. The competition was judged by some of the most outstanding singers of that era, including Antonio Chacón, Manuel Torre and Pastora Pavón. This competition did little to save cante jondo from its downslide, although it did bring to the attention of the public a twelve-year-old boy by the name of Manuel Ortega, who some years later would become the legendary Manolo Caracol.

In 1926, it was decided that a second golden key should be awarded, although some people believed that this award was a farce because many of the great singers of that time were overlooked. The honour went to a singer by the name of Manuel Vallejo.

Born in Seville in 1891, Manuel Vallejo took part in the *Copla Pavón* competition in 1925, and won first prize, which was awarded to him by Antonio Chacón. One year later, Vallejo entered the competition for a second time and it was said that he should have won, but the organisers decided it would not be appropriate for him to win the trophy for a second year running. A compromise was reached, and Vallejo was awarded the second golden key later that year by Manuel Torre in the *Pavón Theatre* in Seville.

During the 1930s and '40s, the cante jondo was fast becoming obsolete, mainly because the flamenco was taken into the theatre: opera flamenco was born, while Gypsy flamenco seemed to be sliding into annihilation. The top flamenco dancers formed troupes, which travelled around Spain performing shows, normally based on the works of Manuel de Falla and Federico García Lorca. These shows were staged in theatres and bullrings, and the companies consisted of a collection of dancers and one or more singers and guitarists.

Another aspect in flamenco's decline was due to the Spanish Civil War, which wreaked havoc on the country between 1936 and 1939. This was a time when many of Spain's top artistes, including a good crop of its flamencos, fled the impending fascist regime in preference for South America. Some, like the guitarist, Sabicas, never returned to live in Spain, but most returned after the war, or after the regime had pardoned them.

The arrival of the 1950s saw a renewed interest in cante jondo, and in 1956, a competition was held in Córdoba, the first of its kind since the 1922 competition in Granada.

In 1957 the first flamenco festival was held in Utrera, and this was followed by festivals in other Andalusian towns, giving local artistes the chance to perform for the public. Artistes from the small towns like Lebrija, Morón de la Frontera, Alcalá de Gaudaira and Utrera were again making names for themselves.

Between the years of 1956-1977, flamenco entered another important stage in its history that in some ways can be considered its second golden age. Many will put the reason for this renewed interest in the hands of the singer Antonio Mairena.

Antonio Cruz García was born in Mairena de Alcor (Seville) on the 7th September 1909, and he is considered among the most formidable flamenco singers of all time. Like Franconetti before him, Antonio Mairena was a singer of great knowledge and affection for the orthodox styles of song. Born into a vast Gypsy-flamenco family, Mairena grew up in the surroundings of his family's blacksmiths, and he was inspired by singers like Joaquín de la Paula and El Niño Gloria.

He desired to perform in the competition in Granada in 1922, but was forbidden from taking part by his father due to the family's lack of money, and the fact that he was just thirteen years of age at the time.

He appeared on stage for the first time in 1924 in a competition in Alcalá de Guadaíra, another important flamenco enclave in the province of Seville. He won first prize in the siguiriya and soleá sections.

At the early stages of his career, he was known as El Niño de Rafael, but by 1930, he had become 'El Niño de Mairena'. He dabbled with flamenco opera, but this was not for him, and so he dedicated his efforts to the festivals that were held in Seville's Alameda de Hércules district, at that time the epitome of the city's flamenco activity.

He was approached by the phenomenal dancer, Carmen Amaya, who asked him to accompany her on a tour of America, but Mairena declined the offer, preferring to stay in Seville, although he did accompany her on other occasions when she returned to Spain.

He became much in demand by the flamenco dancers because of his enormous command of the rhythm and his profound knowledge of flamenco song. He appeared with Pastora Imperio in Madrid and also toured with Antonio El Bailarín, which gave him the recognition that would eventually lead to him being awarded the third coveted golden key of flamenco.

The key was awarded in 1962 and, unlike El Nitri or Manuel Vallejo, whom many believe were not justified in receiving this accolade, Mairena was recognised for his outstanding knowledge of the cante, his enormous contribution to the art of flamenco and, of course, his incredible voice.

Antonio Mairena was responsible reviving many old and forgotten styles of cante, and he amassed an encyclopaedic knowledge of them. He discovered, and was a great admirer of, Juan Talega, a singer from Alacalá de Guadaíra who possessed what best described the orthodox flamenco voice. Talega was living in Dos Hermanas at the time, and from him, Mairena accumulated many old styles of siguiriyas and deblas. Many flamencologists believe that if it were not for the efforts of Mairena, numerous old flamenco styles would have been lost and forgotten forever.

Unlike many of the previous generations of singers, about whom we rely on the words of the writers to give us an insight into their magical powers, Mairena recorded many discs, his first in 1939.

He also turned his hand to *flamencology* (flamenco theory) and together with the poet, Ricardo Molina, wrote what is considered to be the flamenco bible, *Mundos y Formas del Cante Flamenco.*

He remained active in the world of flamenco for the remainder of his life, not on the commercial scene promoted by the theatres and clubs, but in *juergas* and festivals. He dedicated his life to the promotion of the Gypsy cantes, although he was well versed in all styles of flamenco, probably, with maybe the exception of Fosforito, more than anyone else of the twentieth century. He excelled in the lesser-known styles such as toñas, deblas, carceleras and martinetes, and his powerful, versatile voice also lent itself well to bulerías, tangos and fandangos.

The town where Antonio Mairena was born is something of a shrine to the memory of the singer. Other towns in Andalusia have clubs, festivals and monuments dedicated to different artistes, but in Mairena de Alcor, just about everything has Antonio's name attached to it.

He also had two brothers, Manuel and Curro, who were both confident flamenco singers, but their names have been overshadowed by their brother.

Antonio died in his place of birth in September 1983, and today in the 21st century, his talent is still remembered fondly. There is little question in the minds of flamenco aficionados that Antonio Mairena was one of the greatest singers that ever lived.

The 1960s paved the way for a new interest in Andalusia: plane loads of tourists began arriving from all over the world in search of a warm climate, cheap wine and a slice of Andalusian tradition. Flamenco, with its colour, mystical powers and seductive dancing *gitanas*, was the perfect thing to satisfy them.

General Franco's government soon realised flamenco's potential because it appeared that the tourists could not get enough of it.

Suddenly commercial flamenco clubs were sprouting up in major towns, and especially along the Costa del Sol, to give these new visitors their fix of authentic Andalusian tradition. Unfortunately, cheap labour was hired in these clubs so the standard of flamenco was not good. The main objective was to extract money from unsuspecting tourists. The tourists believed they were experiencing a genuine Andalusian art, and they were prepared to pay. While Antonio Mairena was doing his best to preserve this age-old tradition, the tablaos, like the café cantantes before them, were destroying the art beyond recognition again.

During the late 1960s and early '70s, flamenco embarked on a radical change of direction once again.

A meeting between the legendary guitarist Paco de Lucía and a young flamenco singer by the name of Camarón de la Isla was about to turn the flamenco scene on its head. Their partnership was to be another important stage in the history of flamenco. Together they altered and changed the rules of flamenco by inventing new styles and re-structuring old ones, and they went on to become the most exciting thing that had happened to flamenco in a long time. Camarón de la Isla was to become the most imitated singer in flamenco history, and hordes of youngsters looked to him as a god, as he was the first and nearest thing that they had had to a flamenco idol of rock star status.

Camarón de la Isla was to lead the new era of flamenco fusion, and his versatile gitano voice melded perfectly with different styles of world music. He also recorded a disc with the Royal Philharmonic Orchestra - *Soy Gitano*, which secured his position as one of the innovators of the 'new flamenco' movement.

Suddenly, scores of young flamenco artistes appeared, most in the style of Camarón, and the 1980s and '90s was a period when 'new flamenco' performed by artistes like Remedios Amaya and Ketama dominated the charts in Spain.

Camarón de la Isla died in 1992, and nine years later, he was posthumously awarded the fourth golden key of flamenco, because his voice was still very much alive, as it still is today.

His life, which was dogged by drug and alcohol addiction, was preserved in the movie, *Camarón*: its release in 2005 resulted in a new interest and a new army of fans, which has helped keep the legend alive in the 21st century.

Today, there is room for both styles of flamenco, and while the fusion and new flamenco has earned its place in music history, the more orthodox form of this art is again receiving much attention.

Outside its natural surroundings, orthodox flamenco can appear dull, even false. For many aficionados of flamenco, the choice of an old tavern, or the backroom of a bodega, where one can enjoy a glass of *fino* while watching some good old-fashioned flamenco, would be far more appealing than the modern theatres which are used today. The theatres and concert halls are too formal and restrict the audience from joining in and enjoying the flamenco. Audience participation is an important component, as we shall see.

Let's take, for example, the flamenco festivals that are supposed to convey the true atmosphere of the art. Many of the festivals have been moved from open fields or bullrings and re-housed in modern auditoriums. Hence the atmosphere of a moonlit sky and relaxed ambience of a warm summer's night has been replaced by cinema-style seating in modern halls where drinks are forbidden and participation is impossible. Not an ideal setting for any music festival.

Of course, today's flamenco has radically changed and although pretty girls wearing colourful *trajes gitanas* and young men in cordovan hats have become symbolic of Andalusia, these have little to do with the authentic side of flamenco.

One thing one must remember is that all music that has this name attached sprouted from an old tradition that originated in the small villages of Andalusia many hundreds of years ago.

That which is Gypsy

In nothing can the character of a people be read with greater certainty and exactness than in its songs. George Borrow.

The myths and legends that surround the Gypsy race have confused and baffled historians for decades, and many conflicting theories have been born out of misinterpretation and lack of factual evidence. The Gypsies are a mysterious people whose existence has been met with mixed feelings of fear, hatred, revulsion and even fascination.

But where did they come from and why did they leave their homeland in the first place?

Little documentation exists on the Gypsies and theories abound as to where they actually came from. The word Gypsy covers a huge number of different ethnic groups whose existence is evident in India, North Africa, Europe and America. It was first thought that this nomadic race had come from Egypt, a theory that was backed by the Gypsies themselves, as they spoke of Little Egypt, a land they had been driven from by Turkish invaders.

The Gypsies first arrived in Spain in 1425 in groups of around one hundred, led by individuals calling themselves dukes or counts. It is believed that these 'dukes' invented their titles in order to be well received by the leaders of the countries through which they travelled.

Around the year of 1480, another band of Gypsies commanded by captains appeared in Spain, only this time they professed to originate from Greece. Although it is now known that both of these clans, or tribes, of Gypsies originated from the same stock, it was first believed that they were of different origins. The 'Greeks' were generally blacksmiths, while the 'Egyptians' were associated with horse and cattle trading. At that time, it was only noted as to where a particular clan of Gypsies had arrived from. There were no historic records of their travels, and their history was an oral one, so in time the origins of these people were simply forgotten.

One fanciful theory was that the Gypsies of southern Spain were relatives of the ancient *Gaunches*, the people of the Canary Islands. According to their own oral tradition, the Gaunches were driven from Europe around three thousand years ago and arrived on the islands just off the North West coast of Africa, where they lived in cave dwellings. They have also been described as the last survivors of Atlantis.

Another eccentric hypothesis is that the gitanos (Spanish and French Gypsies) are descendants of the Native American Indians. This theory was supported by a 19th century poet, who, after meeting the Sioux chief, Sitting Bull, was overwhelmed by the similarities between the local Gypsies and the Sioux.

There is also the question of what has been termed the 'Baetica Gypsies'. Baetica was a Roman province in the south of the Iberian

Peninsula, an area that included Andalusia. Some writers on this subject have claimed that the Andalusian Gypsies are from a different origin to the Romany Gypsies, and that they arrived here in the eighth century, many years before the Romany Gypsies descended on the shores of Spain. There is, however, no evidence to support this claim.

One of my favourite theories on the origins and fate of the Gypsies is that they were the people responsible for forging the nails used in the crucifixion of Christ, thus doomed to a life of eternal wandering.

Today it is commonly accepted that the Romany evolved from Rajasthan in Northern India. These people travelled from India, through Persia, Armenia and Turkey, and from here, the migration split. Some then went on to Europe, while the others went to Arabia and Northern Africa.

It is known that the Gypsies spent a considerable amount of time in Persia, as their language, Romany, is dotted with many Persian loan-words. It was the Romany language that gave linguists an insight as to where these people had come from, because the Romany language is based on the Indian Sanskrit.

Today, it is still unknown exactly why they started their mass exodus. One interesting legend tells the story of King Bahram, who ruled Persia in the early fifth century. It is said that he was appalled that the lower classes of his kingdom could not celebrate festivities because they could not afford the extortionate fees charged by the musicians. So, he wrote to his brother-in-law, King Shankal of Kannauj (North India). The king reacted to his brother-in-law's plea by sending approximately 12,000 musicians from his land. King Bahram gave them donkeys, cattle, and grain so they could support themselves, only asking in return that they performed free of charge for the underprivileged people of his kingdom.

Approximately one year later, these people returned to the king without food, cattle or any means of supporting themselves. They had spent their time simply playing their music and had squandered their livestock and grain. Furious that they had not sewn the grain and supported themselves wisely, he banished them from his kingdom into a life of perpetual wandering, with only their instruments as a means of making a living. These people were known as *Zott,* an Arabic term used to designate Gypsies.

Music has always played a central role in the lives of the Gypsies and history shows us that they have been professional musicians since the fifth century. They have also made a vast contribution to the music of the countries through which they have travelled. One example of this is the Gypsy musician and composer Janos Bihari, who collaborated in the composition of the *Rakóczi March*, which later became the Hungarian national anthem.

It is also known that the Gypsy musicians played an important role in the propagation of Oriental instruments throughout the Arab world and

Europe. These professional musicians travelled around performing their wild music at weddings, christenings and celebrations of all kinds. Travelling Gypsy musicians have performed just about everywhere, especially in central Europe, and this is why the music of countries like Romania and Hungary has 'the Gypsy touch'.

The Gypsy musicians were extremely gifted at interpreting local music and folk songs with their own musical traditions and customs. This is certainly the case where flamenco is concerned.

When the Gypsies began to appear in Andalusia, they were at first ignored by the Inquisition, since they were too poor and lowly to bother about. But they soon became the victims of much hatred and racial abuse, although they somehow managed to retain their identity.

Gypsy history tells of misery and dejection brought on by their rootless lifestyle, lack of morals, unusual traditions and customs, and unwillingness to conform to modern society.

During the fifteenth and eighteenth centuries they were subjected to numerous laws and decrees which were intended to wipe out their existence. But, as the Gypsies have proved, it is impossible to destroy a race of people with aggression and hatred when these people hold in their hearts such a determined will to survive.

Between 1499 and 1780 many laws were passed in an attempt to eradicate the Gypsy race. The first idea was to banish them from Spain in a similar way to the Moors, but it was likely that they would return when the authorities of wherever they were sent got tired of their presence.

Consequently, they were given sixty days to stop their wanderings and forced to settle into local communities. Failure to do so resulted in imprisonment. They were to settle and live in the same manner as the rest of the population, although under the close scrutiny of the authorities. Laws also forbade them to work in any trade other than agriculture: they were banned from working as blacksmiths, or owning and trading horses, which were two of the Gypsy's main trades.

The wearing of Gypsy-style attire was forbidden, as was conversing in caló, and they were prohibited from performing their wild music and dance.

The arrival of the 18th century saw a different approach to the problem of what to do with the Gypsies. In 1783, a new law, which was to be the last law concerning the Spanish Gypsies, was signed by King Charles III of Spain. Even though this new law still banned the Gypsy way of life, it gave them more freedom to choose where they lived and by what trade they made their living. It was still illegal to wander, wear Gypsy costume or speak the language, and those who continuously disobeyed these conditions would be condemned to death.

These people were no longer to be referred to as Gypsies: instead, they were to be known as 'New Castillians'. This law granted the Gypsies equal rights with other Spanish citizens, especially where work was concerned, and anyone who refused to employ a Gypsy without just cause would be severely punished. This is the reason why the Gypsies of Andalusia are more settled into society than in any other country in Europe.

The life of the Gypsies has been coloured with deep sorrow and unhappiness, dejection and heart-rending grief, along with wild despair. However, their reputation as gifted musicians has always been highly regarded. Their music has had an undeniable impact on the traditional music of the regions where they have settled, so much so, in some cases, it has become their own. Some academics believe that cante jondo evolved from the persecution of the Moors, Jews, and Gypsies, although it is generally perceived to have been the sole creation of the gitanos.

Many of these huge Gypsy clans can be traced back to the times when the settlements first took place in the 15th century. Records from when these families began to arrive in lower Andalusia show that the majority were blacksmiths, sheep shearers, weavers, farm labourers and butchers. These occupations were the main trades of the Moors, and it is believed that the Gypsies took them up when the Moors were expelled from Spain.

If one studies the families connected with flamenco, they will notice that the names of Montoya, Peña, Soto, Monje, Ortega, Jiménez, Fernández and Vargas are amongst the most popular. These families have been associated with flamenco music for centuries and if one studies their genealogical lines, they will see that they assimilate one huge family, connected by the Gypsy ritual of marrying only those of Romany blood.

These families are still producing the most established performers of flamenco, and although their surnames are synonymous with this art, most of the artistes are known only by their nicknames. Most of these names are passed down through the ranks, while others are received because of a particular trait. Andalusians certainly have a penchant for inventing nicknames.

Peña is the name attached to one of the biggest clans, which originated in Lebrija and Utrera. This clan includes the mythical El Pinini, La Fernanda de Utrera, and her sister, La Bernarda, Inés and Pedro Bácan, Miguel El Funi and Pepa de Benito, some of the most influential names of the last century.

This family also has connections with the family of Paco la Luz, whose ranks include El Sordera de Jerez, Luis El Zambo and José Mercé, to name a few.

The name Montoya is another noble name and includes the guitar maestro Ramon Montoya, as well as the family of the great dancer El Farruco, and the singer El Chocolate. The earliest recorded singer in the history of flamenco, Tío Luis el de la Juliana, also had the surname of Montoya.

Ortega was the surname of Camarón's great uncle, Manolo Caracol, whose huge family produced plentiful flamenco performers, such as Enrique and Rita Ortega, along with bullfighters like Rafael and Joselito el Gallo. This branch of the Ortega family also has links to El Planeta, Curro Dulce, Enrique el Mellizo and La Niña de los Peines.

As this demonstrates, and this is merely the tip of the iceberg, the majority of the most prolific flamenco performers in two-hundred years of documentation have been predominately Gypsy. Many of these are related either by blood or marriage, and it is for this reason that the most accepted theory is that flamenco, or certainly the cante jondo, is the product and creation of the Gypsies. The fact that they have preserved and performed this art in the confines of their homes in the small towns and villages in the lower regions of Andalusia for hundreds of years makes flamenco more theirs than anyone else's.

There are many people who dismiss that flamenco is a product of the Gypsies, instead asserting that is a creation of the Andalusian people.

One irate Gypsy singer once told me that 'Those who do not believe that flamenco is of Gypsy origin must also believe that blues is not the music of the negroes.'

Both arguments have substance, and whether one believes flamenco was created by the melding of Arabic, Jewish and Romany culture, or that it is a purely Andalusian Gypsy custom, it is certainly the latter who have preserved the most orthodox style of this art.

A little more than two hundred years ago, flamenco was considered a music that was not worthy of serious consideration, just a wailing mass of noise performed by a bunch of riff-raff. If it were not through the determined efforts of this 'riff-raff', it could quite possibly have disappeared.

If one is fortunate enough to witness an ageing Gypsy singer who has the ability to transmit duende to his audience, then one will, like myself, most probably prefer the mastery of the Gypsy flamenco.

As the words of an old soleá declare: 'That which is Gypsy is found in the surge of blood and the grooves of the hand.'

An Englishman's obsession

I have been exposed to numerous theories concerning the actual meaning of the word flamenco, for it does not refer to just the music and dance. 'A way of life' has been often voiced, and this is probably the most accurate description of them all. This 'way of life' has obviously changed over the last fifty years, and it is true that the old flamenco lifestyle has almost disappeared and will never be repeated, but for many aficionados, it is still part of their daily routine.

When I first discovered flamenco, I became obsessed with the desire to learn everything I could about it. I searched through second-hand bookshops and libraries in the hope of furthering my knowledge. This was a little harder than one might imagine, as, at the time, there was very little on the subject available in English.

Slowly I began to understand this art that I had fallen in love with, but the thing I found very frustrating was not being able to talk to other English-speaking people about this fantastic culture. I found that most flamenco fans either knew very little about the subject, or they were fans of the late Camarón de la Isla, and that was where their interest ended. It's sad to say, but except for the hardened flamenco enthusiasts, the general public, and this includes the Spanish, has little knowledge of flamenco.

To the majority of people, flamenco is dance, the cante being too primitive or monotonous on the ear. One of the most antiquated flamenco voices I have ever heard belongs to Juana la del Pipa. Her delivery is so primitive, and so utterly Gypsy, uninitiated foreigners find it too coarse.

I have seen her perform on numerous occasions, including several times with her nephew, Antonio El Pipa. The name Pipa was handed down by the family's patriarch (also Antonio), who was a vendor of sunflower seeds - *pipas*. Juana is one of the old school of singers whose art is deeply rooted in tradition, and even though she performs in the theatres with her nephew's flamenco troupe, her style of singing is one of the most orthodox and genuine around today.

I was told that I would have difficulties breaking into the orthodox world of flamenco, as it was almost a closed shop to outsiders. For sure, the Gypsies would not want to share their secret with a foreigner, especially an English one. This, to an extent, was true, but more because I was not being taken seriously. Why would an Englishman be interested not only in flamenco, but in the Andalusian Gypsy way of life?

I realised after a while that much of what I was being told about flamenco was incorrect, but not because I was English and being misled, but because the average Spaniard knew very little about the subject also.

This was when it became an obsession. I had been a performing musician for many years in England and I had experimented with many genres. The rhythms used in flamenco, (the twelve-beat cycle is unique to the art form) are a lot more complicated than those of Western style music, but as I am a drummer, I thought I'd be halfway there already. How wrong I was. Only slowly did I start to work out the rhythms and this made it a little easier to distinguish between the different song styles.

The best way to experience flamenco is not in a tablao or theatre, but during a spontaneous performance. Sadly, these are a very rare privilege today, but if one is lucky enough to encounter one, they will see, possibly without enjoyment, how different the two are. To encounter a sudden outburst of song from the people is, be it in a bar or during a family celebration, a very uplifting, even an emotional, experience.

Andalusians like to sing and they love to dance, and whether it be a group of teenagers walking along the street in harmony, or just someone who is inspired to sing for whatever reason, it can happen anywhere and at any time.

One old, overweight Gypsy, who lives opposite my apartment, often bursts into to song, and this is instigated by anything from the food her family is about to eat, to the arrival of her latest grandchild, of which she has many.

I was also informed that if one doesn't understand or speak Spanish, then it would be impossible to understand flamenco. Certainly, you won't understand the words, and this is part of the driving force of the song, although you could still appreciate flamenco. True, once I started to learn Spanish it became a little easier, but when one considers that most songs are a mixture of Andalusian (which is not the same as *castellano*) and caló, the Gypsy language from the Indian Sanskrit, it didn't make that much difference from the enjoyment point of view. In some ways, it can be compared to opera in that you might not understand it, but you can still enjoy it to a certain extent. However, the more you can understand the better the appreciation you will have.

I once took an English friend to a recital by a Málaga singer called Rocío Bazan. Her only previous contact with flamenco had been at a tablao on the Costa del Sol. I explained that this would be completely different. While Rocío performed a soleá, my companion found it impossible to control her emotions: she felt great sadness, but also incredible joy. Tears flowed, but her expression showed pure happiness. She explained afterwards that she did not understand a word of what Rocío was singing, but that she felt as if she had been touched by something - possibly the duende? This is another subject that is shrouded in mystery.

Roughly translated, duende means possession, fairy or even angel. The poet, Federico García Lorca, said, 'Duende could only be present when one sensed that death was possible.' There is no doubt that this phenomenon has been given a very magical and mysterious meaning by poets and writers alike. I think that possession is probably the best description.

Duende can only be present at a juerga or private flamenco gathering: this is another common belief. Personally, I think it depends on what one believes duende to be. I believe it is a state of mind that one reaches while listening to a particular piece of music that touches them profoundly. It is also a state of mind the artiste reaches while performing. It is possible to reach that level when performing in a small intimate surrounding, but it is not so likely to be experienced in a large impersonal concert hall.

Duende is just as likely to be experienced after the consumption of alcohol. This is highlighted by Federico García Lorca's description of the singer Pastora Pavón (La Niña de los Peines). Of her, Lorca wrote, 'At first, she sang beautifully, but had left the audience unmoved. Only later after drinking half a bottle of *aguardiente* did she begin to hold everyone's attention, singing with scorched throat, without voice, without breath or colour, but with duende.'

I was at first led to believe that only those of Gypsy blood could understand and successfully perform flamenco. It is my personal belief that Gypsy dancers possess more *compás* and grace than non-Gypsies, but this does not necessarily mean that you have to be Gypsy to perform good flamenco. Many Gypsies acknowledge the fact that *gachós* are quite capable of performing good flamenco, although they fiercely defend their art as their own creation.

Some of the most influential flamenco artistes ever, like Paco de Lucía, and Don Antonio Chacón, were not of Gypsy blood. The guitarist Sabicas wasn't even from Andalusia; another qualification that is necessary if one believes everything they hear.

The flamenco dancer, El Carrete, told me that it doesn't matter if you are 'English, Spanish, Japanese or Chinese', anyone can learn and perform flamenco dance, and El Carrete is a Gypsy. Given the hugely popular flamenco scene in Japan, perhaps he's right.

The Gypsy guitarist Tomatito said, 'Gachós have a different approach to music. The most important things to a Gypsy are rhythm and expression, but there is an ideal balance between Gypsies and gachós, without which, flamenco could not exist.'

Today there is a rather lucrative flamenco-fusion scene, something which Tomatito helped create, and some of the art's most orthodox performers have been lured into a commercial scene that produces catchy pop songs with flamenco rhythms. The reason for their change from orthodox to commercial is simply the big money that is to be made from it. Flamenco performers can now earn as much money as any other rock or pop star, and some have become the faces of top fashion houses and fragrance brands.

Flamenco and its performers have become big business, but there are artistes like Fosforito who have avoided this commercial scene in favour of orthodox flamenco.

There are, of course, artistes who float between the two. Some critics say that once performers stray into new flamenco, or fusion, they can never return to orthodox flamenco, but this is also unfounded. There are, of course, those who don't want to return for whatever reason, be it the lure of big bucks, or the rock star status that now goes hand in hand with the flamenco scene.

Diego el Cigala has fused flamenco with different styles of music: one example is the CD, *Lágrimas Negras,* where his coarse Gypsy voice sits well with the Cuban jazz style of pianist Bebo Valdes. The album is a benchmark, because the two play together wonderfully.

One singer who has received much criticism from the purists for venturing outside of the acceptable flamenco boundaries is José Mercé. This Gypsy singer from Jerez de la Frontera is capable of producing the purest jondo flamenco because he descends from the huge clan of Paco La Luz. He has been accused of selling out, and maybe, to a certain extent, he has, but he still works the festival circuit, and to watch him with Moraito Chico on guitar is pure ecstasy for any lover of flamenco.

Not being a great fan of new flamenco, I turned my interest in the direction of the orthodox styles. At first, I found it difficult to distinguish between the many different song styles, as there are upwards of fifty. Once I was able to recognise some of them (which is not an easy task for any novice), I started to appreciate what I was trying to understand. This was something that took a while, especially considering that there are many different song families, and within these families, many different variations.

Within the fandango family for example, there are the verdiales, *fandango locales, fandangos de Huelva, rondeñas,* malagueñas, *jaberas, granaínas, fandangos personales* and *fandangos grandes.* The fandangos are believed to have originated in the province of Málaga, although today every region has its own variation of it.

The verdiales come from Los Verdiales, an olive-farming region in the mountains that surround Málaga. Although they are not strictly flamenco, they are the prototype of the fandango. This ancient song form is Málaga's version of the sevillana, and is sung and danced at summer fairs as well as at local fiestas in the mountains, especially in La Axarquía, Valle del Guadalhorce, and Montes de Málaga.

Like the sevillanas, they can be danced by couples and groups, but unlike the sevillanas, they can also be danced solo.

The verdiales have a Moorish feel with melodies similar to those found in Arabic songs. They are performed by a group of musicians known as a *Panda de Verdiales,* who play guitars, violins, and an assortment of percussion instruments. The dancers dress in a colourful and folksy way, with small cymbals on their fingers, and coloured ribbons attached to their hats and clothes. On the 28th of December, the province of Málaga holds its annual Verdiales Festival, and groups of musicians and dancers from different areas of Málaga take part in this unusual, but traditional, gathering of folklore dance.

To the outsider, especially the English, they can resemble the Morris dancers that we either loved or loathed at village fêtes in England.

The origins of Morris dancing seem to have been lost in history, however, it is believed that it was a pre-Christian fertility or luck-bringing dance. The waving handkerchief wards off evil and the high jumps encourage the crops to grow. Over the years, pagan dances such as these have been incorporated into the Catholic and Protestant churches, although many of them have kept their authenticity and have not changed for thousands of years.

There have been many theories as to the origin of Morris dancing, but two in particular are of interest. One is that Morris dancing came from Spain at the time of the Moorish occupation, although there seems to be no certified evidence to support this. The second is that the Morris dance came from Flanders during the reign of Edward III, when many English noblemen and their soldiers were stationed there.

Morris dancing was banned on many occasions by acts of parliament and by the clergy for being too rowdy. Dancers were usually manual workers or farm labourers who performed at village fairs and fêtes, and this provided a chance for the disadvantaged to dress up and be noticed.

The flamenco trinity

There is an area in Andalusia known as the trinity of flamenco, or the 'Golden Triangle', as it is often referred. The three points of the triangle are Triana, Jerez de la Frontera, and Cádiz, and nearly all the major song styles are believed to have originated from this area. It is within this triangle of land that some of the greatest flamenco has been produced by legendary performers who seem to have a superior knowledge of the art, and the majority of these are Gypsies.

Many of the older Gypsy dancers can produce duende with ease, and during what might be just a few seconds of bliss, one will witness something that most academically trained dancers lack.

Much the same can be said about the song. This is endorsed with legendary characters like Manuel Torre, Enrique El Mellizo, Paco La Luz, La Paquera de Jerez and Chano Lobato, all of whom were born in the province of Cádiz

Cádiz, which is still surrounded by part of the old defensive wall that was erected in the 18th century, is one of the region's most beautiful coastal towns. It is also said by many flamencologists to have been the place where flamenco song began, although natives of Triana and the environs of Seville will tell a different story. One thing that is for certain is that the province of Cádiz, especially Jerez de la Frontera, has produced some of the most illustrious flamenco performers in the history of the art.

The district of Santa María is the neighbourhood in which Enrique El Mellizo was born. This Gypsy singer, who created his own personal style of malagueña, was the first flamenco singer to perform a *saeta* to the images of the Passion during Semana Santa.

But how is it possible that after more than one hundred years since El Mellizo's death, his incredible talent is paramount in the research of flamencologists trying to piece together the history of this complicated art? Considering that Enrique El Mellizo was never recorded, and that there is no one alive today who can claim to have listened to him first hand, one would think it impossible to lay such importance on his contribution. It is claimed that he took to singing the styles of Cádiz and improved them with his own creativity, drawing his inspirations from diverse sources, including the Gregorian chant. He has been described as the most prolific creator of song in flamenco history, and also the greatest singer of the styles of Cádiz: many will state that he was one of the greatest singers of all.

He is said to have been the mentor of many singers who followed, namely Manuel Torre and Antonio Chacon. Manuel Torre was said to have been overwhelmed by El Mellizo's singing, especially his malagueñas.

Even today's artistes still perform, or claim to perform, El Mellizo's cante, which is surely testimony to the power he possessed and the amazing impact he has had on flamenco song.

El Gloria was another singer from Cádiz, and he is credited with the invention of the flamenco Christmas carol, the *villancico;* and his style of the saeta is still sung today, as are the *fandangos de Gloria.*

La Perla de Cádiz was considered one of the greatest female singers of Cádiz, specialising in the alegrías, cantiñas and festive songs. She performed in many of the tablaos of Seville and Cádiz, and was noted for her scorched throat.

My personal favourite artiste from Cádiz is the town's predilect son, Chano Lobato. Born in 1927, he is one of flamenco's masters, especially with the cantiñas and alegrías, styles that evolved in the very heart of Cádiz. He spent his early years performing in the taverns and bars of his native Cádiz, where he was to meet La Perla de Cádiz and Aurelio Sellés, the latter from whom Chano would learn his art.

He has performed alongside many of the most elite dancers and guitarists in the business, and his solid sense of compás made him a popular *fiestero*, always full of energy and spirit. He was a master of the alegrías, which are lively and fresh, his torn voice twisting its way around the trotting rhythm. During his long professional career, he was always a favourite with the flamenco dancers, favoured for his solid command of the rhythm and his knowledge of all flamenco styles. This made him popular, and a regular performer, with the Seville dancer Matilde Coral.

He appeared in the 1949 film *Duende y Misterios del Flamenco* alongside La Fernanda and La Bernarda de Utrera, and he also worked with the dancer Antonio el Bailarín for a period of sixteen years.

In 1953, he won the second *Concurso Nacional de Cante,* and in 1974, the Enrique el Mellizo trophy in the *Concurso Nacional de Córdoba.*

Rancapino is another revered singer to come from this part of the triangle. Alonso Núñez Núñez was born in Chiclana de la Frontera (Cádiz), in 1945, where he grew up learning the styles of flamenco song in the streets. In his early teens, he met Camarón de la Isla, with whom he became close a friend, and they performed together in the *Venta de Vargas,* a tavern that has since become a shrine to Camarón.

I saw Rancapino at a festival in Torremolinos, and his voice was like fire and water; the emotion is forced out in surges, tearing at the heartstrings of the listener. He is considered one of the great masters of Cádiz flamenco, and watching him perform his song on this occasion, it is easy to understand why.

Cádiz has been the birthplace of a never-ending list of flamenco artistes, but it will be Camarón de la Isla that springs to mind for the younger generation. It was in the streets of San Fernando that a young Camarón dreamed of being a bullfighter, a career he never entered but in the circle of which he first started to sing flamenco.

He was nicknamed Camarón because his pale-coloured skin and his fragile build, which caused people to liken him to the famous white shrimps of the Bay of Cádiz, *los camarones*.

The town of San Fernando, situated 15 kilometres from Cádiz, is one of the most popular destinations for the avid flamenco aficionado. The town is the birthplace of several celebrated flamencos, including Chato de la Isla, Niña Pastori and Sara Baras, but it is not these artistes that the hordes flock to seek.

With time on my hands during a visit to Cádiz, I decided to head off to San Fernando to see what all the fuss was about. I began my tour at the cemetery and I had no trouble finding the grandeur mausoleum. I must admit to feeling somewhat overwhelmed by the sheer size of this tomb, which is adorned with a life-size statue of Camarón seated under a marble arch. The tomb is covered with votive offerings left by his army of fans. This quiet corner of the cemetery emanates a strange, even eerie, ambience, but I suppose one feels this often when visiting the final resting place of someone of his stature.

My next stop was the small white-washed house in Calle del Carmen where the young Camarón grew up during the 1950s. The house is now a small museum, complete with the bed that the youngster supposedly slept in. The patio was once the scene of nightly juergas, and the walls will have absorbed the cante of numerous great singers, including Manolo Caracol. The area around this street, especially the marshland at the far end, has changed little since Camarón and his best friend

Rancapino used to play here. Much the same can be said of the tiny blacksmith workshop where his father earned a living to support his family. The walls are lined with numerous tools and equipment that his father used to ply his trade, while singing martinetes and siguiriyas. The people of San Fernando seem to have done their utmost to keep the legend of Camarón de la Isla alive, and the Gypsies, most of whom claim to have known him, are keen to discuss his music. Strangely enough, Camarón's music is played in the main street (Calle Real) continuously throughout the day.

The final stop of my tour, for I was in need of some much-needed refreshment, was the Venta de Vargas, the world-famous tavern where the young singer began his career. As might be expected, this place is a shrine to the town's favourite son and the countless other legends that performed here, and although this establishment has seen several alterations since it's golden days, one senses that they are in one of the meccas of the flamenco world.

A bronze statue of the singer was erected in front of the tavern (aptly named Plaza Camarón de la Isla) in 1992, when he was declared Hijo Pedilecto. The statue shows the singer seated on a traditional highbacked chair. In front of him is a figure of a small child, supposedly the young José Monje Cruz staring up at the legend he became.

Unfortunately, the Peña Camarón de la Isla was closed when I visited, but I would image it is yet another shrine to what many Andalusian

Gypsies consider the greatest flamenco singer of all time. Whether one believes this - for it is a matter of much debate - is immaterial, because anyone who is interested in the life of Camarón will not be disappointed by what they find in San Fernando.

Born José Monje Cruz on the 5 December 1950, Camarón de la Isla earned the title of the greatest flamenco singer that ever lived. His death in 1992 gave the Andalusian Gypsies their first deity, and the scenes that unfolded during his funeral, and the aftermath that followed, were surreal. News of his death vibrated around Spain and gripped the nation in a similar manner to when Franco had died 17 years previous, however, unlike the dictator, Camarón de la Isla, who was just forty-one when he died, was about to become a martyr.

Within hours of the sad news of his passing, Spain would witness an extraordinary outpouring of grief, and the people of San Fernando entered a period of uncontrolled lamentation. One hundred thousand people attended his funeral and the riotous scenes that took place outside of the cemetery in San Fernando appeared on the front pages of newspapers around the world.

The Spanish newspaper, El Pais, dubbed Camarón the 'Picasso of flamenco song'; the French press crowned him the 'Mick Jagger' of flamenco. His image became as recognisable as Che Guevara, or even Jesus Christ. Camarón may well have been dead, but a Gypsy martyr was about to be born.

Camarón de la Isla began life as a humble Gypsy who had an incredible command of the flamenco song, and this is what his legend concerns, not the commotion that followed his untimely death.

He made his first record in 1969, accompanied by the guitar of Antonio Arenas, but it was an introduction to a young Paco de Lucía that would launch him on the road to international stardom. Their partnership was to be a milestone in the history of flamenco, because they altered and changed the rules of the art. His early work with Paco de Lucía produced some of the finest flamenco ever recorded, and his later albums with Tomatito paved the way for a revolutionary new flamenco style that would gain him a rock-legend status in the eyes of the younger generation.

Camarón chose to experiment with his music and he was a pioneer in the new flamenco trend.

His 1979 recording, Leyenda del Tiempo (legend of the times), combined musical elements and instruments that changed the course of flamenco as it was known at that time. This album was the first to use the sitar in flamenco, and along with the addition of drums, keyboards and the electric bass, gave a fresh new approach to a once antiquated artform. Camarón had brought flamenco into the mainstream and the youngsters could not get enough. The writer José Manuel Gamboa dubbed the album 'the Sgt Peppers of flamenco'.

Leyenda, like the Beatles' iconic 1967 recording, owed much of its creativity to ground-breaking recording studio techniques and mind-bending drugs, and it initiated the flamenco revolution.

Unlike Sgt Peppers, Leyenda sold less than 6,000 copies when it was first released. There are stories of some fans returning the record and demanding a refund, because Camarón had strayed too far from orthodox flamenco.

The recording, however, directly influenced the future of flamenco and produced a movement known as Camaroneros - dozens of rising artistes who sang in the style of the shrimp from the isle.

Unfortunately for Camarón, like so many artistes of great worth, much of the recognition of his art came only after his death.

In 1993, Camarón's widow, La Chispa, received an honour on behalf of her husband that many people felt should have been awarded while he was still alive. The late singer had been bestowed the title of Hijo Predelicto, the town's favourite son, and a large bronze statue was erected in front of the Venta de Vargas.

There would be ripples among the flamenco sector some years later, when it was suggested that Camarón should posthumously receive the coveted Golden Key of Flamenco. Until then, only three people had been awarded this key.

Pressure had been mounting to honour Camarón with flamenco's highest award, but there were those who questioned why he was not considered while he was still alive. The suggestion of a controversial posthumous award prompted immediate negative reactions, because the key is a symbol of controlling and safeguarding the quality of the cante. A band of detractors argued that the key could not be awarded to anyone who is unable to defend these concepts; an act that would have been previously unthinkable. This all fell on death ears of course, and Camarón was awarded the fourth key in 2000.

Two years later, Camarón would again be the subject of much speculation, when the drive to have him considered for sainthood gathered momentum. Camarón's image was now moving away from a revolutionary Gypsy singer to be replaced by a Gypsy martyr, and although he has yet to receive such a holy order, many Andalusian Gypsies certainly believe that he deserves it.

He began to acquire this image while still alive, and even one reporter who interviewed him near the end of his life claimed she 'thought she was looking at Jesus Christ'.

The reporter, who worked for the El Pais newspaper, also said: 'He (Camarón) radiates something magic, bordering on the realm of the occult.'

There were those who were convinced that he actually had the power to heal the sick, and it became a regular occurrence for him to be asked to lay his hands on a terminally ill child. Camarón apparently found this extremely hard to cope with and he was said to have been bewildered as to why the Gypsies considered him in this way.

On one occasion, when a distraught mother approached the singer to request his help, Camarón, emotionally distressed, asked, 'How am I going to cure him?' He then innocently kissed the child on the head, and this was enough for the press and, of course, the Gypsy community, to add fuel to the myth.

The seeds of flamenco song

Cádiz is one of the cradles of flamenco and it can boast of the importance it has played in its history, but probably the most important part of the triangle is a town located 30 kilometres from the city, Jerez de la Frontera.

Jerez de la Frontera is one of the most majestic areas connected to flamenco. This old Phoenician town was known as Xeres by the Romans, and received the suffix of 'de la Frontera' because it marked the western frontier of Moorish Kingdom of Granada.

Jerez is famous for its fortified wines and sherries, and its dancing horses, but it is also one of the greatest producers of Gypsy flamenco in all of Andalusia. The two flamenco districts are those of San Miguel and El Barrio de Santiago.

Of all the towns and villages that I have visited in my quest for flamenco knowledge, Jerez is by far the most wonderful of them all.

The huge church of San Miguel towers above the old cobbled streets that were once the scene of regular impromptu flamenco sessions. This district has constant reminders of people like the mighty Manuel Torre and Don Antonio Chacon, who were both natives of the area. Peñas and flamenco taverns bear the names of these masters, and also of many others who made San Miguel one of the most respected areas of flamenco in the early part of 20th century.

The *Peña Antonio Chacón* is tucked away in the corner of a small junction.

Antonio Chacón García, born in 1869, was one of the masters of flamenco song and also one of the most important figures in the creation and preservation of it. Antonio Chacón was not of Gypsy blood and his voice was not afillá: instead, he had a cleaner, higher pitched voice that was more suited to cante andaluz.

He astounded his Gypsy companions with his vast knowledge of their song styles, but, with his clean falsetto voice, it soon became obvious that he was not well suited to this style of flamenco.

He spent his childhood in his father's shoe shop in Jerez, the place where he met the guitarist Javier Molina, and these two would go on to forge a partnership without comparison.

Against the will of his parents, he started to frequent the taverns and local juergas, and at the age of fourteen, he received his first break with the help of the Enrique el Mellizo.

El Mellizo, who was astounded by Chacón's talent, convinced his father that the boy should accompany him to Cádiz to perform in the café cantantes. The youngster was paid the sum of seven pesetas a night for his efforts. He was later hired by the *Café Burrero* in Seville, and soon began to etch his name on the café cantante scene. He was next hired by Silverio Franconetti to perform in the *Café Silverio*, and he was also a regular performer in the celebrated *Café de Chinitas* in Málaga.

He became a master of many styles due mainly to his acquaintance with Enrique el Mellizo, who gave him an excellent source on which to base his creations. He is credited with the creation of the *Granaina* and the *cartagenera*, both of which he derived from the fandango.

Chacón became known as the gentleman cantaor because of his dignified and passive nature, and he was the first singer to use grammatically correct Spanish in the words of his songs. Prior to this, a mixture of Gypsy and Andalusian slang had been traditionally used in the lyrics of flamenco.

Chacón and Molina travelled around Andalusia studying the different styles of flamenco. They visited some of the most obscure villages in search of diverse forms of cante that were in danger of extinction, reviving many old styles that had long been overshadowed by the commercial scene.

In 1922, Chacón formed part of the jury that presided over the *Concurso de Cante Jondo* that was held in the grounds of the Alhambra Palace in Granada.

His dislike of phonographic records resulted in him only recording four records; this was done when his health and fame were fading, so these recordings apparently do not show his full potential.

He became one of the most educated singers of his era, drawing his knowledge from his journeys around Andalusia. He eventually achieved such refinement with his flamenco that the prefix of 'Don' was attached to his name, which in those times was strictly reserved for those of blue blood. To this day, Don Antonio Chacón remains the only flamenco artiste to have received this honour.

He has been referred to as the greatest flamenco singer that ever lived, but it is fact that Chacón was far surpassed by other Gypsy singers in the cante gitano. It may be fairer to say that Chacón was the greatest singer of cante andaluz, the style in which he excelled and to which his voice was far more suited.

He died in poverty in Madrid in 1929.

Another of the great legendary singers from San Miguel was Francisca Méndez Garrido, La Paquera de Jerez. Born in Calle Cerro Fuerte, in 1934, it was to be in Madrid that La Paquera made her name, rubbing shoulders with the top artistes of the time.

In 1971 she was awarded the *Niña de los Peines* trophy at the Córdoba *Concurso Nacional de Cante Flamenco,* and she gained the title of the 'Queen of the Bulerías'. She sang bulerías and soleares with the force of a volcano, while her tientos and fandangos were executed with that indefinable art of the Gypsies of Jerez.

La Paquera was *cuchichi*, a half-Gypsy, but she possessed a quality that only the Gypsies seem to be able to inject into their flamenco.

During the early period of her career, under the guidance of her cousin, Diego Rubichi, La Paquera sang in the municipal market, and in the abattoirs and forges, which, only a few years before, had been the stomping grounds of Manuel Torres and Don Antonio Chacón.

During her colourful career she has worked with many guitarists of Jerez, including the brothers Manuel and Juan Morao, but her favourite accompanist was Parrilla de Jerez. She stormed through the festival circuit of the 1960s and '70s, her emotion-charged, duende producing voice astounding all that experienced it.

She died at the age of seventy in Jerez de la Frontera in 2004.

The most nostalgic area of Jerez de la Frontera is the Barrio de Santiago, the old Gypsy district that remains much the same today as it has always been. In these dilapidated streets huge Gypsy dynasties cultivated their flamenco. There are some specialists who insist that the very first seeds of flamenco singing were sown in the streets of Santiago, especially in Calle Nueva and Los Carpenteros.

Terremoto de Jerez, El Sordera, Maria Soleá and El Borrico are just a few of the mighty singers that have made this area so regal as far as flamenco is concerned. This tranquil district is still home to many of today's artistes, most of whom descend from the clan of Paco La Luz.

Paco la Luz was the patriarch of a family whose members are still at the front of the flamenco scene today. This family includes Luis el Zambo, one of the most orthodox singers of the Jerez styles; and

Parrilla de Jerez, a respected guitarist, who was a regular accompanist of Tía Anica La Piriñaca.

Ana Blanco Soto, La Piriñaca, descended from a family whose roots were firmly embedded in the world of bullfighting and flamenco. She had two brothers, one a singer of flamenco, the other a bullfighter. She was not pure Gypsy, although she had Gypsy blood on her father's side.

She never sang professionally until late in her life because her husband disliked her singing, but, following his death, she dedicated the last years of her life to singing flamenco. It was Antonio Mairena who noticed her ancient quality, and he persuaded her to record her voice for posterity. Previous to this, La Piriñaca had only sung in taverns, normally with the singer El Borrico. She was a singer who knew well the most antiquated songs, although she recorded only a few tracks during her short career.

It is with these old dames of flamenco that the most authentic side of the art can be appreciated. She will be remembered as the rounded old Gypsy with a voice like granite, especially when singing the siguiriyas, soleares and bulerías.

She died in Jerez de la Frontera in 1987.

The mighty El Sordera de Jerez was another prolific singer whose repertoire was broad, and he was the first gypsy distinguished with the title of Favourite Son of Jerez.

His children, which include Sorderito, founder member of the fusion group *Ketama,* and flamenco singer Vicente Soto, are continuing their father's legacy, as are his countless nephews, which include José Mercé.

Born José Soto Soto in 1955, José Mercé grew up in the area of Santiago, and he acquired his stage name of Mercé from the *Basilica de Merced*, as he sang in the church's choir.

As a child, he lived with his uncle, El Sordera de Jerez, which is where he developed his understanding of the flamenco song. Other influences came from relations like Tío Borrico, another legendary singer born in Jerez de la Frontera in1910.

José Mercé's family is also connected to that of the El Terremoto, which links his name to most of the large Gypsy flamenco population of the neighbourhood of Santiago. He is also related to the clan of El Pinini, another huge flamenco dynasty whose roots stretch from Jerez to Lebrija and Utrera.

José Mercé cut his teeth singing in the tablaos and taverns around Cádiz and Seville, but it was to be Madrid where he would embark on a career that would send him to the very top of his profession. His first job in the capital was at *Torres Bermejas,* where he would meet and perform with artistes like Camarón de la Isla and Paco de Lucía. After this, he undertook a ten-year contract with the controversial flamenco dancer Antonio Gades, and this would take him all over the world.

He also appeared on screen with Antonio Gades and Cristina Hoyo in Carlos Saura's adaptation of Federico Garcia Lorca's *Bodas de Sangre* (Blood Wedding). In 1995, Carlos Saura called on him again to appear in his film *Flamenco,* during which he performed with Manuela Carrasco.

José Mercé's first few recordings are pure cante jondo, and on these he demonstrates his encyclopaedic knowledge of the orthodox styles.

Today, he is one of the country's top flamenco artistes, famed for his voz afillá, a dry, husky voice full of a passion and emotion that is synonymous with Gypsy singers. But he also advocates bringing flamenco to the youngsters, and his fresh approach to flamenco has made him an artiste of the masses.

We must not forget the wealth of flamenco guitarists and dancers that hail from Jerez de la Frontera. These include Perico el de Lunar and Javier Molina, two of the most inspirational guitarists, and the Moraos, whose legacy has been continued by several decedents.

The list of dancers is endless and includes La Sordita, daughter of Paco la Luz; La Malena, who was still dancing at the age of eighty-two; and La Gamba, the first wife of Manuel Torre.

Tia Juana la del Pipa was an enormously overweight woman who was capable of letting rip with a duende-filled display of dance, especially with her bulerías, which were full of suggestive and provocative movements.

Even today, the flamenco dance is dominated by the offspring of the Gypsies of Jerez: Joaquin Grillo and Antonio el Pipa are proof of this.

The forges of Triana

I remember how old and nostalgic Triana appeared on my first visit. I was excited because I had heard so much about the district, and I longed to see if it had retained any of the old flamenco atmosphere.

This quiet district, situated on the west bank of the river Guadalquivir, was once home to countless renowned Gypsy bullfighters and flamenco performers, and it is saturated in myths and legends concerning these two arts.

As I walked over the Puente de Isabel II (the Triana bridge) the first thing that greeted me was the monument to flamenco. The bronze statue was erected by the town hall and bears a plaque that reads, *Triana Al Arte Flamenco.*

The streets that run parallel with the river - Calle Betis and Calle Puerza - are where one will begin to understand the ambience of this old district. The houses in these quiet streets are adorned with ceramic plaques remembering illustrious writers and poets, courageous bullfighters and celebrated flamenco singers that were born or lived there during the golden age.

I knew that years before it had been the very centre of flamenco song, and even though the legendary flamencos had long departed, it still had an antiquated ambience that separated it from its neighbour on the opposite side of the river. These streets once echoed with the sound of flamenco song, and even though this had also evaporated with the times, it felt as though it had been absorbed into the streets and buildings. I tried to imagine what it would have been like in the golden years, but the flamenco way of life in Triana had truly passed. These nostalgic times have, unfortunately, been replaced by the hubbub of a modern day Triana that bears little resemblance to its golden age.

It must be remembered that many of the artistes of those days did not have the pop star status of today's performers. Most lived in poverty or very close to it. They needed to sing to provide food for their families. The singers would spend long evenings in bars hoping to be hired for one of the juergas. These parties would normally go on all night, after which, everyone would move on to another venue to continue the festivities; most often spending whatever they had earned by sunrise.

This way of life has long disappeared and the flamenco is now centred on a few bars like *La Anselma*, a flamenco tavern that is owned by the dancer whose name it bears.

La Anselma, a former professional artiste, was born and raised in the streets of this old flamenco neighbourhood. The club is housed in a typical 18th century house with tiled exterior and boxed balconies. The club offers a scheduled show comprising the lighter styles of flamenco and folk dances. However, don't go too early, because nothing happens until around midnight.

Today, Triana's up-market image is supported by yuppie flats, modern tapas bars and night clubs: one of the only things that is still sacred to Triana is its ceramic industry.

Of course, during the late 19th and early 20th centuries, it was the flamenco capital of Andalusia. Many of the local Gypsies worked in the forges, and it was these blacksmiths who have been attributed with the invention of the martinetes, a song style which they used only their hammer to beat out the rhythm of the song. El Planeta worked in the forges of Triana and he is thought to be one of the main contributors to the Triana school of cante.

One of his pupils, Diego el Fillo, also worked as a blacksmith in Triana, and these two singers, among the first in flamenco's badly-documented history, are thought to have played a major role in the creation of the flamenco deep songs.

La Andonda, who was reputed to have been married to Diego el Fillo, was said to have been born in Triana, although another version of her life states Utrera as her birthplace. One thing for sure is that she spent much time in Triana, possibly because of her romance with El Fillo.

La Andonda was said to have a violent and unbalanced nature, so much so, she would often engage in street brawls with anyone who would fight with her. This was normally after drinking excessive amounts of alcohol, after which, she would release her anger with soleares filled with rage and fury.

One of the most important names during this era in Triana is that of Los Caganchos, three brothers who were part of El Fillo's family tree, and who are said to have been legends in their own time.

Antonio, Joaquin and Manuel were born in Triana in the second half of the 19th century and, according to local lore, they rarely left Triana, seldom even crossing the bridge into Seville. All were blacksmiths, and because they were brought up in the family's forge in Triana, the siguiriyas and martinetes were second nature to them.

The most celebrated of the three was Manuel, whose siguiriyas were said to be primitive and completely without ornamentation. The brothers only ever performed for a close group of friends, who would congregate in the back room of a small grocery store to hear them sing their wonderful cante. They never accepted money for their performances, and their only reward for singing was to witness the reactions of these listeners, who are said to have behaved in the strangest ways while they performed.

Juan Pelao was another famed singer from this period famed for his wonderful martinets. He was born in Triana in 1845 and was closely associated with the Caganchos. He lived through the café cantante period, but was never tempted to sing commercially or for money, and he refused his singing to anyone who was not of Gypsy blood.

Fernando el de Triana, born in 1870, was another popular local singer who had a wide repertoire. He was said to be a spontaneous creator of song and also played the guitar, but was most remembered for a book he wrote called *Arte y Artistas Flamencos,* an invaluable look into the flamenco scene of the late 19th and early 20th century.

Naranjito de Triana, born in Calle Fabíe in 1933, was another of Triana's famous sons, although his flamenco was more commercial than that normally associated with Triana.

The building that now stands on the site of the house where he was born is decorated with a plaque commemorating his life's achievements, which included leaping out of a huge cake during Evita Perón's visit to Seville. Another was his professional partnership with Narci Díaz, which has often been compared to the artistic partnership of Manolo Caracol and Lola Flores.

He performed with many of the great flamenco guitarists, including Sabicas, Juan Habichuela, and Paco de Lucía, with whom he recorded a *bambera* to the rhythm of a soleá por bulerías. This was the first time that this had been done, although it was rejected by the dyed-in-the-wool aficionados.

Aside from its famed singers, Triana boasts a few dancers who have played an equal role in securing its rightful position in the golden triangle. El Faico is remembered as a fine Gypsy dancer of the *farruca,* and he impressed audiences in Russia with his dance during World War One. He also spent time in Paris, where he had considerable success, but he was to return to Spain a broken man after his wife ran off with an admirer.

Felipe de Triana was also a famed dancer, although not professional. He was said to possess that 'evasive something that is the very nucleus of flamenco'. He also performed with the Gypsy dancer, Juan el Tumba, and together they would perform at private juergas, delighting their audiences with their natural Gypsy *gracia*.

Another of Triana's sons who made good was the dancer Antonio de Triana, remembered as a phenomenal dancer. Antonio left Spain to work in America, where he performed in numerous films, as did his daughter, Luisa de Triana.

But Triana is equally as famous for its bullfighters, many of whom were born in Calle Betis, the riverside street which offers panoramic of the *Maestranza* bullring. One of these was Juan Belmonte, a courageous man whose career was the stuff of legend. His life's achievements have been recognised with an unusual bronze sculpture, which is located in Plaza Altozano.

Born into abject poverty, Belmonte invented a technique that brought him much closer to the bull's horns than earlier matadors had dared, even though he was born with a deformity in one of his legs. He broke every accepted rule and paid the penalty repeatedly, but he did not die in the ring: instead, after being diagnosed with terminal lung cancer, he took his own life in Utrera in 1962.

Many specialists I had talked to on my quest for flamenco knowledge had described flamenco as the sister art to the bullfight, and I wondered what the two had in common. According to the family tree of Manolo Caracol, which is littered with flamencos and bullfighters, quite a lot, it seems.

For the Gypsies, flamenco and the bullfight were the two means of which a reasonable living could be made, and also a way of making a name for themselves.

The bullfight is another predominant aspect of life in Seville, although many find it too barbaric to actually witness first hand. These two arts definitely have a connection as far as the tourists are concerned. A tacky plastic flamenco doll or a black plastic bull with two *banderillas* dangling from its neck are among the most popular souvenirs bought by tourists.

Many of the bullrings were used during the opera flamenco era of the 1940s, and many are still used for festivals today. I know of people, mainly Brits, who refuse to enter a bullring even to attend a flamenco festival simply because of what takes place in them on a Sunday afternoon.

Lorca's Granada

In the early hours of Wednesday 19 August 1936, a military truck trundled up through the winding roads of the Vega de Granada and on to an unknown location, where one of the most atrocious crimes of the Spanish Civil War took place. The world-renowned Spanish poet and playwright, Federico García Lorca, was a passenger on the truck and, along with three other condemned men who were also on board, he was never seen again. The death of Lorca caused outcry, and poets and writers from around the globe condemned the Franco regime for such a disgraceful waste of human life. Talking about the murder, Chilean poet Pablo Neruda declared, 'We will never be able to forget this crime, nor forgive it; we will never put it out of our minds and never will we excuse it, never.'

The death of Lorca, who was considered one of the greatest names of modern European literature, became an increasing embarrassment for the regime, and they sought desperately to exonerate themselves in the eyes of world opinion. When it became clear that fault did not lie with the Republicans, the Nationalist propagandists laid the blame on unspecified assassins.

It is unclear why Lorca was arrested, and theories abound concerning his homosexuality, but it is of general opinion that the poet was targeted for his outspoken socialist views. He demanded justice for people of all races and origins, edging closer to active political involvement, even though he considered himself apolitical. In 1933, Lorca made his position on fascism clear by adding his name to a manifesto condemning the Nazi persecution of German writers; and later, he would openly voice his support for the Popular Front, a coalition founded in January 1936 by the main Spanish left parties. He signed several documents in connection with the imprisonment of prominent figures, the Brazilian Communist leader, Carlos Prestes, being one of them: he also joined a society called 'Friends of Latin America', an organisation dedicated to the struggle against dictatorships.

In the months leading to the Spanish Civil War, politics and the arts had become entangled, and political significance was given to the words and actions of influential writers like Lorca.

Federico García Lorca, who claimed flamenco was the 'greatest creation of the Spanish people', was born in Fuente Vaqueros, Granada, in 1898. His work focused on Gypsies, bullfighting, flamenco, archangels, landscape, love and death. One of his most acclaimed (and longest) poems (*Llanto por Ignacio Sánchez Mejías*) is a tribute to his friend Ignacio Sánchez Mejías, a bullfighter killed in the ring in June 1934.

His book, *Romancero Gitano (Gypsy Ballads),* published in 1928, became the most popular book in Spain at that time, although Lorca declared that he wrote the first three ballads purely for his own enjoyment. He described the book as an 'Andalucian altarpiece' that portrayed the olive groves and landscape of his childhood, disturbing memories of the civil guard, archangels and, of course, Gypsies.

It was with this collection of poems that Lorca's poetic countenance appeared for the first time, and it was declared his most ingenious work to date. Critics hailed Lorca as the greatest Spanish poet since Antonio Machado, and copies of *Gypsy Ballads* sold out within weeks of the first publication.

Unlike many of his generation, who treated Gypsies with contempt, Lorca saw as them as 'the truest and purest thing in Andalusia'. His passion for their flamenco was further endorsed by *Poema del cante jondo* (poem of the deep song), which consists of 55 poems grouped into ten sections. The poems are dedicated to styles such as siguiriya, saeta, petenera and soleá, and the theme of most of them is death, frustrated love, heartache and despair.

The words of many of Lorca's poems have been used in flamenco song, and most of his plays have been brought to the theatres by flamenco troupes, *Bodas de Sangre* being one of the most popular.

Several flamenco artistes have dedicated whole albums to Lorca's work. The Granada-born singer, Enrique Morente, recorded an album named *Morente-Lorca - Campanas por el poeta* (bells for the poet). The recording is an excellent melding of Morente's Arabic-style chant, accompanied by a choir and the clanging of cathedral's bells. Very un-flamenco, one may think, but Morente's unique voice captures the very essence of Lorca, and Granada, the city he so loved.

Granada, which boasts one of the oldest flamenco peñas in Andalusia, *Peña La Plateria,* was the last city to fall to the Catholic Monarchs, ending nearly eight hundred years of Muslim rule. To the Gypsies, it will always be *meligrana,* caló for pomegranate - Granada.

When one thinks of Granada, one of the most prevalent images that springs to mind is the colossal Alhambra Palace, set to a backdrop of the snow-capped Sierra Nevada.

My first visit to this magnificent Moorish fortress is secured firmly in my mind. It was a spring morning and my first glimpse of this eighth wonder was slightly distorted through the foggy mist that covered the mountains.

Known by the Moors as the *Bermejo castle,* in reference to the red clay bricks that were used in its construction, it is the oldest Muslim palace in the world, and certainly one of the most beautiful.

Described by Manuel Machado as 'hidden water' that pours out like tears, Granada, especially the Alhambra, has inspired the works of numerous writers, poets, and artists over the years. One was Washington Irving, who lived in the crumbling old palace for several months during the 19th century while writing *Tales of the Alhambra*, a collection of stories and legends about the palace and its inhabitants. But Granada has more to offer than its the Moorish palace.

The Albaicín was once the heart of Muslim Granada, but the Gypsies moved into the district after their expulsion. This area was popular with the 19th century romantic writers, most of who were fascinated by the Gypsies that lived in the caves. These charcoal Gypsy beauties performed a mysterious music and erotic dance that mesmerised many foreign travellers.

However, George Borrow gave a different description, saying that Granada was the poorest city in Spain, and that the Gypsies were 'truly miserable, with the greater part of them living in beggary and nakedness'.

Today, the Gypsies are still to be found here, offering their art to the many tourists who flock to the area in hope of catching a glimpse of what the romantics experienced. Much of this area has been given over to tourism, and the flamenco that is presented today is a far cry from the flamenco that was performed here in the 19th century.

Granada, like Málaga, is not known for producing an abundance of pioneering flamenco singers, at least not to the standard of places like Jerez de la Frontera, but it has played an important role in the history of the art: the province is credited with several flamenco styles, such as the *zambra,* a style that originated in the Sacramonte cave district. Like the alboreá, *mosca and cachuchas,* the zambra, which derives from the Arabic for music, *zámara,* was performed during Gypsy wedding celebrations.

The *romances* are connected to Granada through the works of Lorca. Many of the lyrics to these songs are taken from *Romancero Gitano*. The poet is also credited with the creation of the *lorqueñas,* a style similar to the bulería made famous by artists such as La Argentinita. The granaína is a style of fandango associated with Granada, although many experts attribute its creation to Don Antonio Chacón. One of its greatest interpreters was Enrique Morente, born in Granada 1942. This controversial singer was often criticised for venturing outside the accepted flamenco boundaries. His adoration of Don Antonio Chacón is evident in his style of delivery, but he also experimented by fusing flamenco with rock and Indian music, which mortified the dyed-in-wool aficionados. He does, however, have a unique flamenco voice, which he demonstrates on recordings like *Morente-Sabicas*.

Another singer famed for the granaína was Frasquito Yerbagüena. Born in Granada in 1883, he was also credited with the creation of the *abandolao*, a style of fandango. He was known as the goldfinch, a reference to his voice, for which he won five hundred pesetas in the 1922 Concurso de Cante Jondo.

A festival of dirty straw hats

'Nothing more than a festival full of dirty straw hats, shabby clothes, and performed by a bunch of riff raff.' This was the reaction of one of the many people opposing the *Concurso de Cante Jondo* that was held in Granada in 1922. Some of the upper-crust of Granada felt that flamenco was not an art, but an excuse for a degenerate rabble of undesirables to get together in an orgy of Gypsy-style mayhem.

Regardless of this stance against flamenco, festivals are now celebrated all over Andalusia, and they are excellent gatherings for those who enjoy the orthodox style of this art. The festivals are generally organised by local councils, or flamenco peñas, and are preceded by a flamenco *concurso*, normally for the song. However, in Córdoba, where the first competition was held in 1956, they also hold a guitar competition.

The festivals take place in an open field, a theatre, bullring or playground. These offer typical flamenco atmosphere, while the town's legacy within the art will determine the sort of flamenco one will witness.

Personally, I think the smaller festivals held in towns and villages offer the best ambience, as these are more intimate, especially if there is a local artiste appearing on that night.

I remember well my first festival. I had gone to see José Mercé, who was sharing the stage with Calixto Sánchez, Rancapino and Carmen de la Jarra, among others. I stood through nearly five hours of pure cante: I had arrived too late to get a seat. Did I stay there because I liked what I was listening to? I certainly didn't understand it. The reason was because José Mercé was last on the bill and his music was the only flamenco I was familiar with at that time.

It was while walking home that night that I questioned whether I liked cante jondo, or whether I just like the music of José Mercé. To tell the truth, I found cante jondo a little tedious, it all sounded the same. I remember thinking that they were all singing the same songs. I also remember feeling a little out of place, as if I was somewhere I shouldn't have been.

People had cautioned me to be careful because the audience would be predominantly Gypsy, and I was warned to keep an eye on my wallet. I was feeling a little nervous, not for fear of being robbed by the Gypsies, but because I knew that I was probably one of a very few English people in the audience. Today, these festivals have become the highlight of my summer, especially the *Potaje Gitano* festival in Utrera.

Most major cities, as well as the surrounding towns and villages, hold festivals. Many of the festivals are named after local Andalusian dishes, supposedly highlighting the days of the poverty and hunger of the

Gypsies. For example, *potaje gitano* is a stew of beans and vegetables. *Gazpacho* (cold Andalusian soup) is the name of the festival in Morón de la Frontera; and in Lebrija, *La Caracola* (snails), which, like the other dishes, is traditionally offered to the audience during the festival.

Other festivals are named after the town's most famous artiste, as is the case with the *Festival de Cante Jondo Antonio Mairena*.

Each festival is preceded by a competition inviting singers from all over Andalusia to compete for a first prize of two or three thousand euros and a chance to appear in the upcoming festival alongside some of the more established names.

The festivals usually start around 11pm and continue into the early hours - *la madrugada*. One will need stamina, not only to stand four or five hours of cante jondo, a challenge for even the most hardened fan, but to queue for twenty minutes to buy a ticket, to join another long queue to purchase a drink; and remember, the Spanish never have quite grasped the procedure of queuing!

The Potaje Gitano in Utrera was the first flamenco festival to be held in Spain, and it took place on 15 May 1957, during the town's Easter celebrations. It began shortly after the Gypsy procession had passed through Calle Nueva in the early hours of Good Friday.

The festival was proposed by the Hermandad de los Gitanos de Utrera, and was organized by Andrés Jiménez Ramairez (head of the brotherhood at that time), his brother, Manuel, and various members of the Gypsy community.

The festival's name derives from a large pan of bean stew that had been prepared and offered to the audience during the festival, along with plates of olives and plenty of red wine.

The gathering was held in a small makeshift enclosure. There was no amplification for voice or guitar, and no order of appearance for the artistes. El Cuchara, Gaspar de Utrera and El Perrate de Utrera were the singers chosen for the event, all of whom were accompanied by the guitar of Diego del Gastor.

The event was deemed a success, and so the *Potaje Gitano* festival was born.

In 1958, Antonio Mairena made an appearance, and he also persuaded Juan Talega to perform, an old singer who possessed the most orthodox flamenco voice, and who belonged to the family of Joaquin el de la Paula.

The third festival was overshadowed by the death of José de Aurora (the father of La Fernanda and La Bernarda de Utrera), who had died in the January of 1959, and so the festival was dedicated to him. During this festival, a wooden spoon, which had been signed by Antonio Mairena, was raffled, raising 500 pestetas for the brotherhood.

The list of renowned artistes to adorn the stage continued to grow, and the appearance of Pepe Torre, brother of the celebrated Manuel Torre, during the fourth festival, was again attributed to the insight of Antonio Mairena.

The sisters La Fernanda and Bernarda de Utrera made their debuts in 1961, which was the first year that women had been invited to perform. This was also the year that Antonio Mairena was made an honorary member of the Utrera brotherhood of Gypsies.

Guitarist Diego del Gastor was responsible for introducing some of Morón de la Frontera's flamenco luminaries, such as Andorrano, Anzonini, and Joselero, another upholder of the orthodox styles of song.

Joselero was born in La Puebla de Cazalla, but had spent the majority of his life in Morón de la Frontera. He was a non-professional singer who specialised in the soleares, siguiriyas, bulerías, and the malagueñas of Enrique el Melizo. His son, Andorrano, was also said to have been an exceptional singer.

Anzonini was a non-schooled Gypsy singer and dancer from Cádiz who was said to have been an excellent fiestero. His lineage had Italian and English blood, which gave rise to his intimate nickname of Lord Leighton.

Over the years, the Potaje Gitano festival has presented just about every renowned performer from the 20th and 21st centuries, especially those from Jerez, Utrera, Lebrija and Morón de la Frontera. This festival has paid homage to mythical characters like La Serneta, Rosario de la

Colorao, Manuel Torre, Manolo Caracol, El Pinini and, of course, La Fernanda and La Bernarda.

There is an amusing tale connected to festival of 1968, which refers to the disappearance of the chairs which were hired for the festival. The blame was directed at the local Gypsies, who denied any knowledge of the chairs' whereabouts. Some forty years later, this rather amusing tale was relayed to me in an old bar in Utrera, and even though the narrator claimed the blame did not lie with the Gypsies, smiling, he added, 'however, most of them had new patio furniture that year'.

Andalusia has a lot of good festivals that are held throughout the summer months. Another of my favourites is the *Torre del Cante,* held in Alhaurín de la Torre, Málaga.

Alhaurín de la Torre is not the easiest place to get to on a Saturday night for those without transport, but it would have been worth walking the ten kilometres to see the line-up at the first festival I attended. José Mercé, El Chocolate, Aurora Vargas, Capullo de Jerez, Maríana Cornejo, and that year's competition winner, Gitanillo de Vélez, were on the bill that night.

The old football stadium where El Torre del Cante is held (it has since moved to the Finca El Portón) was packed and the stage was set in typical flamenco style. High-backed Andalusian chairs draped with silk shawls; tables laid with bottles of sherry; while the aroma of jasmine penetrated the night air. There were people from all walks of life. The old, in shawls of numerous designs and colours, fans in motion; while the men congregated at the bar enjoying a glass of fino, not a care for what was going on around them.

I was pleasantly surprised at the number of young people that were in attendance. I mention this because cante jondo is a diminishing genre, so it's particularly nice to see the younger generation enjoying, and hopefully continuing, this wonderful culture.

El Chocolate was 71 when I first saw him perform. Immaculately attired in suit and tie, his silver hair in contrast to his dark chocolate complexion; his ancient, mournful tone is one of the last traditional voices of flamenco. He is a singer who prefers the more orthodox styles and is at his very best with the siguiriyas, soleares and toñas. He is also a master of the style of *taranto* made famous by Manuel Torre, a singer from whom El Chocolate drew his inspiration.

The voice of El Capullo de Jerez is an agonising roar, a voice so haunting, it makes the hairs on one's neck tingle. Awkwardly slouched on his chair, his neck disappearing into his body and his eyes bulging from their sockets, Capullo's style has a very modern feel with heavy rhythms and cutting guitar falsettos, although the power of his *eco gitano* is what has made him one of the most unique singers of his era.

It was around this period, my first full festival season, that I became fascinated with singers like Antonio Mairena, La Fernanda de Utrera, Chano Lobato, El Perrate de Utrera and Juan Talega. I must admit that at first it was a difficult to truly appreciate their art, but I persevered: a little like when you try your first olive. It is an acquired taste, but once you get the flavour, it tends to stay and mature.

Spontaneity, grace, and polka dots

It is commonly perceived that flamenco dance has evolved from the dances of the Hindus. Female flamenco dancers concentrate more on the upper body and arm movements, similar to that of the Indian dance, where the focus is on arm movements and facial expressions. If one watches the dancer, Saray, perform her very personal style of tangos, they will see that she incorporates the upper torso routine similar to that of the Indian dance, while her lower body shows similar movements to those of a belly dancer.

Similarities in the female flamenco dance to those of Indian dance movements, especially those of the upper body and arms, are too noticeable to be ignored. When performed gracefully, the arching of the back and the twisting of the wrists show signs of a connection between the two forms. Consequently, the uninitiated believe that there is a story behind every movement, just as there is in the Indian dance. This is not the case with solo flamenco dance. Outside a commercial setting, the female solo flamenco dancer, for example, does not unfold a story whilst she is dancing, she will only interpret what she feels at that moment, using her style and ability to convey these feelings to her audience.

When two dancers perform together, however, they will often play out a story, usually of love or jealousy or both.

The style of dance we see performed today is considerably different compared to the late 19th century, and styles of flamenco song that were never accompanied by the dance are now being taken up by modern performers striving to find new directions for the flamenco dance.

But what makes a good dancer? Grace, rhythmic skill, duende or simply the ability to perform spontaneous dance? By 'spontaneous', I mean that the dancer will feel the music and dance what he or she feels from the music at that particular moment. The dancer needs to express him or herself and let their personality take grip of the dance, and not just go through the motions of a show that is rehearsed right down to the facial expressions.

There is a phrase that declares, 'When you learn to dance, you must also learn how to forget.' All that a good dancer has been taught must at times be ignored, and the dancer will rely on the wisdom that flows in the blood. The dancer must feel the rhythm of his or her heart beat and let that guide them through the interpretation. With a natural instinct and the knowledge of how to use the rhythm, a brutal mysterious force will be unleashed, while the dancer searches the most inner depths of his or her soul to attain a certain high when the duende fills the dance.

A wonderful dancer who could best demonstrate this was La Chicharrona, an enormously overweight Gypsy dame who would perform her provocative dance routines with her dress pulled high over her knees as she teased her spectators in a way that would make even the men blush. This type of dance will not normally be witnessed in a commercial setting, but it is possible in an intimate surrounding where the person dancing is transformed by the flamenco and unaware of anything around them other than the rhythm of the song.

There are no rigid rules as such in orthodox flamenco dance; the dancer uses whatever technique his or her ability allows, as long as it remains within the boundaries of flamenco. If he or she is dancing *por tango* for example, it will be within the frame and rhythm of the tango, but what is actually danced will be the dancer's interpretation of the tango during that particular performance.

Gracia, compás and duende are all elements that the dancer must possess. A good dancer will not need much room to perform, especially the female, who will concentrate on the upper body and arm movements. The arms will be curved, raised above the head, and then lowered with the palms of the hands facing downwards.

The male's fist will go from being tightly clenched to fingers stretched to the limit, where the female hand movements are more fluid and graceful. It is quite astonishing how the dancer manages to stop so suddenly without losing balance, instead, immediately composing him or herself, and so gracefully.

The facial expression of the dancer will reveal a lot as well. The concentration will be undisturbed, as if oblivious to everything. However, most often the facial expression is false - grinning hideously while dancing, a trait often displayed in tourist tablaos.

Tablao or theatre flamenco will almost certainly be highly choreographed as it would be impossible to have four or five dancers on a stage dancing unpractised without disastrous results. The style one will occasionally witness, with the dancer leaping around the stage, spinning out of control and falling to his knees to receive adoration has nothing to do with pure flamenco dance. The overly flamboyant acrobatics are not part of flamenco, as both feet should never leave the floor at the same time. This style is, unfortunately, the type that is often staged for gullible tourists in search of traditional Andalusian culture while on holiday.

The incredible Gypsy dancer El Farruco was entirely focused on the rhythm and unaware of anything other than his interpretation.

Born Antonio Montoya Flores in 1935, El Farruco spent most of his youth on the open road living the traditional Gypsy existence. His father was a horse and cattle dealer who traded at the fairs and markets of Andalusia, and this is where the youngster cut his teeth, performing with his mother, La Farruca, a Moroccan beauty who was also a competent dancer.

He descended from the great Montoya dynasty, whose members include the guitarist Ramon Montoya, El Farruco`s grandfather.

El Farruco was one of the most unusual dancers of the last century and rarely has a dancer with his physical characteristics created so much genius with the dance. He would stand motionless, almost trancelike, with his arms outstretched, index finger and thumb together, his rugged face tilted under his cordovan hat and his pot belly hanging from below his tight-fitting waistcoat. Then, with a simple twist of his wrist, his arms raised above his head, he would dance some of the purest Gypsy flamenco that one could ever hope to see.

There have been many dancers whose technique and physical attraction would have been far more appealing to foreign audiences. His overweight frame gave the impression that he would probably do as little as possible, as he slowly moved about the stage, faking a turn and snapping his fingers. But in an explosive frenzy that lasted for just a few seconds, he became as if possessed by daemonic forces that controlled his every move. He had a natural animal instinct that had his audience hanging on his every move, and the duende and emotion that filled his dance has rarely been equalled.

He spent much of his life in Seville, where he opened a dance school, a place where many of today's top dancers studied. He travelled the world with different flamenco troupes, including those of Manolo Caracol, Lola Greco and Matilda Coral, and in 1977, joined forces with his daughters under the title of *Los Farrucos*.

The history of flamenco is littered with characters who show us what this art is all about, and none so much as El Farruco. His grandson, Farrucuito, has become one of today's top, if not controversial, stars of flamenco dance.

But it would be impossible to talk about the flamenco dance of the twentieth century without mentioning Carmen Amaya, Vicente

Escudero, and Antonio Gades. These dancers are three of the most important figures in the world of Spanish dance: they are also the three people who helped shape the style of flamenco dance that is most popular today. Many of today's top dancers have studied under, or been influenced by, one of these three extraordinary dancers.

Carmen Amaya, born in Barcelona in 1913, was a Gypsy who was to become one of the most outstanding *bailaoras* of the twentieth century. She was also one of the most imitated.

Her masculine style of dance was often copied, but she was inimitable, and to this day there has never been a dancer to match her ferocious style. Her rattling footwork became her trait, although she is remembered as the dancer who wore the *traje corto*, a tight-fitting suit normally worn by men.

She created a personal style of dance, which, along with her macho image, non-conformist attitude and legs of steel, became her trademark. She revolutionised the female dance and broke many of the rules and traditions of the old-style dance, which attracted much criticism. She was accused of de-feminising the female flamenco dance, which, until then, had concentrated more on the arm and upper torso movements. She danced with a serpent-like ease, and became an icon for thousands of imitators, however, it was not just her dance that made Carmen Amaya imitable, but also her sharp Gypsy wit and unconventional character, which were incorporated into her performance.

She died on the 19th November 1963.

Another dancer that was to make a considerable mark on the history of Spanish dance was Vicente Escudero, quite possibly the most controversial flamenco dancer ever. His refusal to conform to tradition and his disregard of the compás made his style the subject of much debate. It is true that if one does not possess compás, then they will not perform good flamenco, but Vicente Escudero had compás, only he refused to be confined by rules and regulations.

Born in Valladolid in 1887, Escudero began his career in the streets, dancing what he described as his 'dances of life', performing to the rhythm of machinery or anything that produced a beat. It was said that he had little knowledge of the flamenco rhythms, and many guitarists refused to work with him because of this.

Escudero believed that to copy was simply stealing, and he criticised many dancers for not having personality, or the ability to improvise, referring to most of his contemporaries as 'mechanical dancers'. This attitude made him unpopular with other artistes, but the general public loved what he did. The average audience had no idea about compás then, as they still don't today.

Despite his unpopularity amongst other dancers, Escudero was one of the most natural dancers to ever grace the art of flamenco: his stubborn, non-conformist attitude made him the very substance of true flamenco. He was a creator in every sense of the word.

Although he was not Gypsy, he spent much of his early childhood in their company, which is why he had little respect for polished academic dance. He was a strong believer that men should dance as men, as he felt that the male dance had become too effeminate.

He was an admirer of Antonio de Bilbao, but it was his introduction to the dancer La Argentina that was to be his starting point on the route to international stardom. La Argentina was the one who channelled his drive and trained him as an artiste.

Escudero spent the majority of his career outside Spain, because, like many flamenco artistes of this period, his art was little understood in his native land. He loved the avant-garde scene that dominated the artistic life in Paris during the late 1920s, a period when he began producing flamenco-theme drawings and paintings. Many of these sketches can be viewed at the permanent exhibition that is now housed in the Museo del Baile Flamenco in Seville.

He was responsible for developing a high level of sophisticated dance, a dance that did not always conform to the tradition of flamenco, and a style that was, for best part of his artistic life, hugely criticised.

The last of this trio is Antonio Gades, one of the most revolutionary Spanish dancers of the twentieth century. Like many artistes of his era, he was exiled for many years during Franco's rule because of his political stance. He was a communist and a defender of the revolution in Cuba, a country in which he had strong political and personal commitments. Cuban president Fidel Castro acted as his best man when he married the actress, Marisol. When Gades died in 2004, his ashes were interred in the *National Pantheon of Heroes of the Revolution*, a memorial cemetery in Havana, Cuba.

Born in Alicante, Antonio Esteve Ródenas went to live in Madrid at an early age. He was born of non-Gypsy parents and spent his early years working in numerous jobs, including apprentice bullfighter, and a messenger boy for the ABC newspaper, but dance was his calling. He was spotted by Pilar López, who gave him the artistic name of Gades. He worked his way up through the ranks of her flamenco company to eventually become her lead dancer, a position he held for nine years. He learnt many forms of Spanish dance with this company, including classic Spanish dance, and he also took advantage of the lengthy world tours, studying other forms of dance in Russia, Paris, and Italy.

He performed on the most famous stages around the world, travelling extensively with different productions, which included many of Federico García Lorca's works. His dance was a mixture of modernism and ancient flamenco tradition, which won him more awards than any other Spanish dancer to date.

Today, the jondo dancer is a rare sight: what we see in the tablaos and commercial establishments is choreographed dance rather than spontaneous. Vicente Escudero would have frowned upon the commercial dance scene of today, because it goes against everything he stood for.

The most un-flamenco objects used in the tablao dance routines are the castanets. It is a common, but mistaken, belief that the castanets are a flamenco item. These are a fairly recent addition and were introduced to enhance the sound of the finger snapping, and to add another element of interest to the dance in the cafés and tablaos. None of the old and respected dancers like La Chicharrona needed additional props to perfectly perform their art. However, there are some music styles which now fall under the flamenco umbrella that do make use of castanets. True, these forms are outside the jondo frame, but they do have a flamenco feel. The sevillanas are one example. These are the dances you will see performed by most Spaniards at ferias and celebrations throughout Spain, and it would seem that this dance comes naturally to them.

An early experience of the sevillanas occurred in a nightclub in Seville. The music was the typical dance and house variety. Everyone was having a fine time, dancing, drinking and generally having fun. The dance floor was packed with people between the ages of eighteen and forty, when suddenly, the pop music was replaced by a sevillana. What happened next has remained with me ever since. Everyone began to dance in harmony. I watched in amazement. I couldn't believe that everyone knew how to do it. It was so automatic, as if someone had flicked a switch. I remember asking my companion, Javier, how everyone, he included, knew how to do this style of dance. He told me that they grow up with the sevillanas, their mothers dance it, in fact, all the family dance sevillanas. He looked at me in disbelief when I told him that we had nothing of the kind in England.

I asked how he had learned the intricate steps and routines of the sevillana, considering that he had never taken dance lessons. He told me that it was something he had learned in the streets of Seville, watching the children who were privileged enough to be sent to dance school. He would simply imitate what he had seen.

I have seen this man dance on many occasions and although he does not observe the formalists rules of flamenco dance, he has the ability to engage in a dance that is so profound, so spontaneous, it is nothing short of pure flamenco.

Flamenco comes to life in an old tavern or the backroom of a bodega, where the scorched, cracked voice of the singer, combined with the passionate tones of the guitar meld together to create the atmosphere that makes this art so mysterious.

On one occasion in a back street bar in Málaga, a group of flamenco aficionados, which included Javier, got together for an impromptu session. I was accompanied by some English friends who wanted to see the more traditional side of flamenco, and this is exactly what they witnessed.

We arrived at around 11pm, and it was not long before the wine was flowing and the voice of Camarón de la Isla was bellowing from the stereo. Javier, a man the locals refer to as El Sevillano, jumped from his seat to get the party going. He is not a professional dancer, his style is original and primitive, but primitive only as in traditional, not inferior. He prefers, and certainly excels in, the lighter styles such as the sevillanas, tangos, bulerías, and rumbas. Occasionally something will ignite from deep inside of his soul, and on this particular night his fuse had been lit.

I noticed a small guy, perched at the end of the bar who suddenly produced a tatty old guitar from a worn leather case and began to tune it. The bar fell into silence as we waited while he fiddled with his instrument, wriggled himself into position, and then he began to strum a slow and mellow *Tango de Piyayo*. This encouraged El Sevillano back to his feet. Now the juerga was in full swing, and cries of joy rang around the bar, the clapping rhythms and foot stomping drowning out the guitar, but lifting the dancer to an even greater high.

I was overcome by his dance during a bulería, which seemed to engulf me, and for a moment I was lost, seduced by the rhythm and entranced by the ambience. I watched as Javier rose to the tips of his toes, his arms high above his head, fingers snapping to the rhythm. This was utterly flamenco, a happening that lasts for just a few minutes, a happening which leaves one spellbound.

As a child, Javier lived opposite El Farruco. He described him as a short, fat-bellied man whose trousers were always short of his leather ankle boots. He claimed that he would keep an eye out for local youngsters who showed signs of becoming a great flamenco dancer. El Farruco had apparently approached his mother on a few occasions to try to persuade her to bring him to his academy, but Javier's mother refused, preferring him to concentrate on his studies.

The sevillana is a colourful and exciting style of song and dance that originated in Castille, not in Seville. It is a variation from a style of dance known as the *seguidilla*. It is performed to a strict 3/4 rhythm and will be danced by pairs or groups of people to a pre-established routine.

This style of dance is performed at fiestas of all kinds throughout Spain, but especially during the ferias, when women will wear colourful polka-dot dresses that add a swirling character and grace to the dance.

The sevillanas, originally a courting dance, can be very erotic and sensual, although the pair will never touch each other until the final moments, when the man will put his arm around the waist of the woman. Not so many years ago, young Spanish couples were limited in their courting practices: the man would spend the night talking to his *novia* through the iron grills of her door or window, and, if they did get the chance to go for a walk, they would most definitely be chaperoned by the girl's mother, sister, or whole family. The feria week would be one of the only times that the man could show his affection for the girl by asking her to accompany him in the dancing of sevillanas. This is most probably why there is little physical contact, as the whole night would be watched by the prying eyes of the girl's family.

Music and dance are very much part of everyday life in Andalusia, as are the colourful dresses and accessories that accompany them. The female dancer's dress is based on Andalusian street wear of the 19th century, which had hemlines down to the ankles and a tight-fitting waist. With the addition of the long train on the dress, the *bata de cola*, and polka dots of different colours and sizes, the traje de gitana was born.

Today's dresses have more frills, a lower neckline and a higher front or side split. This is all part of the prostitution of flamenco and simply detracts from the dance by the display of leg and cleavage. Furthermore, some of the dresses are so fanciful that they actually restrict the dancer's movements.

It has been my intention to try to explain the difference between traditional flamenco dance performed by non-professionals, and commercial tablao flamenco. One needs to encounter the spontaneous, raw emotion of pure flamenco, and then compare it to the commercial flamenco that dominates today's scene. It is, of course, understandable that many tourists who visit a flamenco tablao while on holiday would prefer to see a pretty young girl in a colourful, suggestive dress cavorting about the stage in preference to an overweight Gypsy who more resembles a barrow-boy than a dancer. But what one must remember is that flamenco is an age-old art that has been preserved by non-professionals, people who have used flamenco as a form of expression.

New flamenco will continue to discover fresh avenues and become even more distant from its original form.

I believe that only the Gypsies will continue with the true form of this art. Unfortunately, the jondo singing and dancing will be something we have to search out, like searching the countryside for a rapidly disappearing form of wildlife.

A rainy day in Utrera

There are certain towns and villages in the lower region of Andalusia which have a special appeal to the lovers of flamenco nostalgia, and none more so than Utrera. This old flamenco town is situated just 30 kilometres outside Seville and it has produced one of the biggest clans of flamenco artists in history. This family, whose patriarch was the mysterious El Pinini, includes La Fernanda and La Bernarda de Utrera, Pepa de Benito, Miguel El Funi and Inés Bacán, to name just a few. Their deep, soulful voices are unique to Utrera and Lebrija, and there are many who would say that these two towns have produced some of the best singers in the history of this art.

Even before I set foot in Utrera, the name had a mystical feel and I knew I had to go to the town to absorb myself in its incredible flamenco tradition. One dark October day in Seville, with time on my hands, I decided I would take the short journey to Utrera. I had read very much about this town, but even this did not prepare me for this delightful experience.

As I stepped off the train, it was very cloudy, in fact it was black, and the heavens were threatening to open. Little rain had fallen since April, but all the signs showed it would be back today with a vengeance.

A short walk from the train station I found Calle Nueva, and it was in this cobbled street, at number twenty, that the sisters, La Fernanda and

La Bernarda de Utrera, were born. The street has changed greatly since they lived there, and today there is nothing left to remind you of them.

Soon the heavens made good their threat, turning the streets into rivers and soaking me to the bone. I didn't particularly care; I was finally in Utrera, and a thunderstorm and torrential rain were not going to dampen my spirits.

The travel writer Michael Jacobs had described Utrera as an ugly town, but what I encountered was anything but ugly. True, the outskirts are a little bleak, but the centre was dripping with history and culture; I suppose it depends on what one is looking for.

Although the 21st century has arrived in Utrera to some degree, much of its antediluvian lifestyle is still evident. The primordial ambience will engulf one from the minute they arrive. The residential back streets are in a state of tranquillity at all times and this serene environment will only be interrupted by the occasional clanging of the church bells or the buzzing exhaust of a scooter. It's predominantly Gypsy charm (they first settled here in 1600) is what makes the town stand out from all others.

The centre of Utrera overflows with heritage. The 14th century Moorish castle, *La Banda Morisca*, is in the very heart of the old town and towers over the old fountain made famous by El Pinini.

Gothic, Baroque and *mudéjar* architecture can be found at every turn in the quiet back streets, and even the flamenco peña is situated in the most picturesque setting, flanked by a patio of orange trees and tranquillity.

There are plenty of things to remind one that they are in one of the most important towns as far as Gypsies and their flamenco is concerned. Many of the old bars have walls lined with photographs of some of the town's most illustrious artistes, and in these old establishments, people are keen to talk about the importance of Utrera's flamenco contribution.

I have found the Andalusian people to be extremely proud, especially where their cultural heritage is concerned, and they will go out of their way to discuss it with anyone who shows an interest.

One place where I experienced this was in the Bar Bética, dedicated to the Real Betis football team. Around small wooden tables old guys in cloth caps played dominoes amidst clouds of cigarette smoke and noise. At first, I got the usual looks to which I have become accustomed, although I think that the first thing that intrigues them is my height, as I tower well above the average Spaniard.

I got chatting to the barman about Tomás de Perrate, prompted by a picture of the singer that was on the wall behind the bar. The barman seemed a little surprised that I knew of this local singer, and when I volunteered that his father, El Perrate, was a master of the art, he asked me how an Englishman could possibly have heard of these singers. I explained that I had lived in Andalusia for the past eleven years and that I had a passion for flamenco. He told me that the best singers came from Utrera, 'the best in all of Andalusia'. To be honest, I think there are many who are of that opinion.

Inevitably, once he realised I was English, he wanted to talk about football. Apparently, Chelsea FC were to play Real Betis the following week in Seville. When I explained that I knew nothing about football, he was even more confused. He turned to his customers and with a loud cry across the bar, blurted out, '¡*Madre mia*! An Englishman who knows nothing of football but has a passion for flamenco, incredible.'

The old guys laughed and agreed, without looking up from their dominoes, as the barman walked away shaking his head with amusement.

It took me a while to find the statue in honour of La Fernanda and La Bernarda, and when I did, I was a little shocked at its location. It has been placed in the middle of a roundabout at a junction opposite the municipal market. For a beautiful town with such an important flamenco tradition, it seems a shame that a better site could not have been found for these divas.

The sisters are an important part of flamenco history, especially La Fernanda, who retired a few years ago due to ill health, but she has left a legacy within flamenco that will be difficult to match.

La Fernanda's sister, Bernarda, is still performing at seventy-eight years of age, and she is one of a few surviving masters of the orthodox Utrera school.

Fernanda Jimenez Peña was born in Calle Nueva in 1923, and she had a powerful voice that blistered with aggressive rage, drenched with the sorrow and pain of her race.

She is the daughter of a simple, but respected, butcher who worked in the abattoir in Utrera, and it is said that he did not want his daughters to become flamenco artistes. He was bemused as to why they would want to sing in taverns and clubs in Madrid when he considered that he earned enough money to support his family. Again, it was the singer Antonio Mairena who realised the priceless quality of flamenco knowledge that these two sisters possessed, and he persuaded their father to let them make a record. This recording was to be the beginning of their long and illustrious commercial careers.

La Fernanda was recognised as 'the queen of the soleares', a style that she was said to have based on the songs of Mercedes La Serneta, even though La Serneta died eleven years before she was born.

La Serneta died in 1912, but her style of soleá has been widely reinvented, although any authenticity is based solely on word of mouth, because La Serneta never recorded anything. One must remember that many of these old styles of flamenco have changed greatly over the years, and some of those that are performed today bear little resemblance to the archaic forms sung in their original structure. One must also remember that many of these old 'masters' spent the majority of their lives in the village or town where they were born. They would probably have only sung for family and a close circle of friends. They were not artistes in the true sense of the word, and would have only sung in their own barrio or district. Their reputation would have been spread by close friends and associates, who carried stories of their genius to places far beyond their community.

La Serneta was an exception, because she spent time performing in Madrid, where it is said that she passed her style of song to Manuel Torre and Tomás Pavón.

Even though La Fernanda based her soleares on those of La Serneta, she injected them with her own personality, so much so that they became known as the *'Soleares de La Fernanda'*.

La Fernanda de Utrera had a special voice that was full of a gravelly emotion similar to that found in the old blues singers like Billie Holliday or Bessie Smith. Singers of flamenco seem to gain a unique quality to their voices with age, and the riper the age the more ardent their voices become. La Fernanda had this special quality and in her later years her voice was a struggling, pain-filled, cry that came straight from the blood in her veins.

Many of these old singers have destroyed their voices with years of singing, smoking and drinking, all ingredients in the preparation of many great singers. But La Fernanda's voice was void of all the body and grit in her later years because of illness, and wear and tear. As a result of these factors, she was left with a chilling echo, a profoundly emotional cry that numbed the body and sent one's hair to a shivering attention.

In her prime, she was majestic, her voice rough and raucous, tearing at the heartstrings and smothering the listener with a warm and glowing duende. She was said to be at her most pleasing in the juerga atmosphere: to see her perform with Diego del Gastor, one of her preferred guitarists, was probably the most rewarding show of flamenco delivery one could ever hope to experience.

She participated in the TVE series, *Rito y Geografia del Cante*, which was recorded during the 1970s, and this is one DVD collection I would recommend to any serious flamenco lover, especially those wanting to experience a typical 'fiesta gitana'. There are many episodes in the series that capture La Fernanda singing on the patio of the old Pinini house in Lebrija, encouraged by members of her huge clan.

Another singer by the name of El Perrate, also born in Utrera, and also an excellent interpreter of the soleares of La Serneta, appears in this flamenco series. He performs with his sister, La Perrata, and one gets the impression that they are speaking in an ancestral language that has been passed down through the centuries, a language that only the Gypsies from the small towns and villages can understand.

This way of life, which has been practised by flamenco dynasties for centuries, has virtually disappeared over time, and, unfortunately, it will never be repeated. The Gypsies of Andalusia have settled into society more so than in any other part of Europe, although there are a few towns, such as Utrera and Lebrija, where the old flamenco way of life still exists.

As I wandered around Utrera in search of its flamenco legacy, it became obvious that the majority of the Gypsies had lived here for generations. Even the likes of La Fernanda and La Bernarda, who took their art to places as far afield as New York, always returned to Utrera, because it was their home.

There is an amusing story that tells of La Fernanda's mother's concern for her girl's first visit to America, because she worried how they would provide for themselves in New York. Obviously, she did not have enough faith in their singing, because she advised them to open a *churro* stall should they fall on hard times.

Of course, the average lifestyle of the Spanish people has changed greatly over the last thirty years, and the poverty and hunger that many of these people suffered is something that is remembered only by the elders.

Also, many of the old Gypsy neighbourhoods have been disbanded and their traditions and customs have receded with them. There are, of course, Gypsies who still live by the law of the Romany, but even these have become more relaxed with time. It was once unthinkable for a Gypsy to marry a gacho, or to work like one, but today the majority do both.

Another interesting thing I learned while in Utrera was that Rita Hayworth's family had connections with the town. Hayworth's real name was Margarita Carmen Cansino, and she was the daughter of a flamenco dancer by the name of Eduardo Cansino: he descended from a family that manufactured Mostachones, a cinnamon-flavoured cake, famous to the area. I soon found a small bakery that sold this sweet delicacy, and promptly brought myself a bagful.

As I left the shop, I noticed on the other side of the street another monument to one of Utrera's past flamenco legends, Enrique Montoya, a singer and guitarist who left his mark on the town's legacy. Along with a successful solo career, he also performed with El Perrate, and another local singer, Curro de Utrera, in a flamenco trio that received much acclaim.

Curro de Utrera, who spent much of his life in Córdoba, had a softer style, not so gravelly, but instantly recognisable because he had that quality which is unique to Utrera.

The street that leads to the flamenco peña, which is named after Curro de Utrera, is lined with delightful white-washed houses. At the end of the street is a huge church (Santa María de la Mesa), opposite which, one will discover the peña, which is tucked away at one end of a small patio dotted with orange trees: the scene is painfully picturesque. One must wander around this maze of tiny, peaceful, streets in order to absorb the time-worn ambience they emit.

During my first trip to Utrera, I learned plentiful stories concerning the town's huge contribution to flamenco, and I was constantly reminded of the mythical El Pinini, Bambino, Gaspar de Utrera, Pepa de Benito, El Perrate, and, of course, La Fernanda and La Bernarda. It is in the back streets of Utrera, especially in Calle Nueva, that one can almost feel the presence of this legacy. The old patios that are hidden behind decaying walls hold many memories of when flamenco was part of everyday life. Some of these old back streets seem to have stood still in time and the only reminder of the 21st century is the style of cars parked in them.

As I left Utrera that afternoon, the sun was shining, and I felt that I had just taken a trip back in time: if only that were possible.

Former home of Silverio Franconetti in Calle Mesón de Moro, in the Santa Cruz district of Seville

Monument to Antonio Mairena,
Paseo de Colón, Seville – Plaque
recording Mairena's birthplace

140

Statue of Manolo Caracol in La Alameda de Hércules, Seviile

Statue of Pastora Pavón (La Niña de los Peines) in La Alameda de Hércules, Seville

142

*Statue in memory of La Fernanda
and La Bernarda, Plaza Ximénez
de Sandoval, Utrera*

143

Statue of Niño Ricardo, Plaza de los Venerables, Santa Cruz, Seville

El Perrate, gardens of the castle in Utrera

Monument in memory of Enrique Montoya, Plaza de la Constitución, Utrera

Bust of El Terromoto de Jerez in Barrio de Santiago, Jerez de la Frontera

Tiled plaque in memory of Diego del Gastor, Calle Diego del Gastor, Morón de la Frontera

Statue of Camarón de la Isla, opposite Venta de Vargas, San Fernando, Cádiz

The Camarón route: his father's blacksmiths (above)
The house where he was born (below)
La Callejuelas district of San Fernando, Cádiz

149

Camarón de la Isla's tomb in the municipal cemetery in San Fernando, Cádiz

Statue of La Perla de Cádiz in
Calle Plocia, Cádiz

151

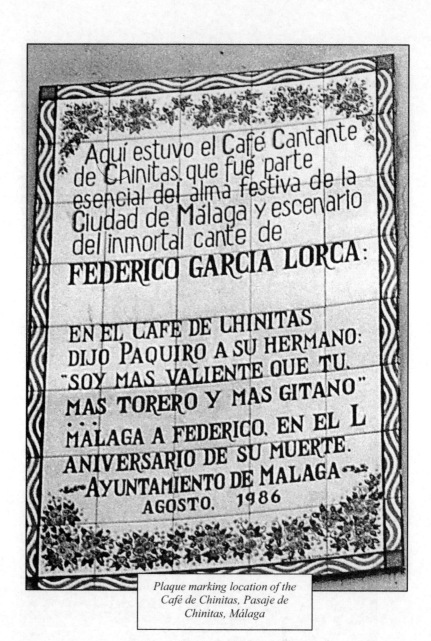

Aquí estuvo el Café Cantante de Chinitas, que fué parte esencial del alma festiva de la Ciudad de Málaga y escenario del inmortal cante de

FEDERICO GARCIA LORCA:

EN EL CAFE DE CHINITAS
DIJO PAQUIRO A SU HERMANO:
"SOY MAS VALIENTE QUE TU,
MAS TORERO Y MAS GITANO"
. . .
MALAGA A FEDERICO. EN EL L
ANIVERSARIO DE SU MUERTE.
AYUNTAMIENTO DE MALAGA
AGOSTO. 1986

Plaque marking location of the Café de Chinitas, Pasaje de Chinitas, Málaga

Mural dedicated to Camarón and Paco de Lucia, Centro Comercial, Torremolinos

EN ESTE NÚMERO DE LA CALLE FABIE NACIÓ EL 12 DE NOVIEMBRE DE 1933 D. JOSÉ SÁNCHEZ BERNAL, NARANJITO DE TRIANA QUIEN COMO RECREADOR Y CONSERVADOR DE LA VIEJA ESCUELA TRIANERA DEL CANTE FLAMENCO, LLEVÓ CON ORGULLO Y DIGNIDAD A TODOS LOS ESCENARIOS DEL MUNDO EL NOMBRE DE TRIANA.

Plaque marking location of the birthplace of Naranja de Triana, Calle Fabie, Triana

Statue dedicated to El Carrete,
Plaza Costa del Sol,
Torremolinos

Lebrija

Lebrija, a small town not far from Jerez de la Frontera, is another of the flamenco territories that is as important as Utrera. Lebrija has a similar appearance to that of Utrera. Narrow winding streets of picturesque houses, which, if you cheekily peer through the doors of, hide beautiful Arabic-style patios tiled in eye-catching mosaics, laden with exotic plants in glazed earthenware pots, with the occasional fountain sleepily trickling away the siesta.

This dusty town sits in the middle of a white hilly landscape, and hosts the second oldest flamenco festival, La Caracola. Even more important are the huge flamenco families from this town, the Peñas, and the Bacáns, families that have direct connections with Utrera. This family's patriarch, El Pinini, is still remembered with fondness by the local people, even though he spent the majority of his life in Utrera.

The incredible singer, Bastián Bacán, one of El Pinini's numerous grandsons, was said to have sung better than Manolo Caracol, although he spent the majority of his life singing in private juergas and the taverns of Lebrija and Utrera. He was the father of guitarist Pedro Bacán, and of one of today's most orthodox singers, Inés Bacán.

Born Inés Peña Peña on the 14th of December 1952 in Lebrija, she spent her childhood in the heart of Lebrija´s Gypsy-flamenco community. Her grandmother, Fernanda La de Funi, although not a professional, was said to have been a singer of great voice.

Inés Bacán was thirty-seven when she first began singing professionally. Before this, she only participated in family celebrations, which would include anyone from La Fernanda to La Perrata and Miguel el Funi. But it was with her devoted brother, Pedro, that she would embark on her professional career. He took her under his wing and they performed together for several years, until, in 1997, he was killed in a car accident in Utrera.

Inés appeared on several discs produced by Pedro called *Noches Gitanas en Lebrija,* and the siblings also appeared together in many shows, not only in Lebrija, but in Germany and France. One of the best-known shows was *El Clan de los Pininis*, which, as the name suggests, included numerous members of this extended family.

Clan is the operative word to describe this huge family, a family whose roots stretch from Jerez de la Frontera to Lebrija, Utrera, and far beyond.

Ine's career was to take a different direction after the death of her brother. She appeared at many festivals and peñas all over Andalusia, as well as at many festivals in France. To date, she has recorded three CDs, one with the Jerezano guitarist Moraito Chico, on which, she demonstrates her skill at singing the traditional styles of Lebrija. She excels in the mournful Gypsy styles like the soleares and tientos, and her cracked echo is so melancholy it hurts.

Another of the town's flamenco legends is singer Juan El Lebrijano, born in 1941. The son of La Perrata, his early years were spent performing in the tablao *El Guarjiro* in Seville, and then in *El Duende,* in Madrid.

Since childhood, he had an incredible wealth of art from which to draw his inspiration. Brother of the renowned guitarist, Pedro Peña, his relatives include Tomasa Torre, daughter of Manuel Torre; La Niña de los Peines, his godmother; Gaspar de Utrera, considered one of finest singers of his era; as well as El Turronero, Inés Bacán and Tomás de Perrate.

He is a singer who continues his family tradition, although he has explored many different avenues with his flamenco, including melding it with *andalusi* music, an area, which, at that time, had not been previously explored. On another recording, he performed with the Moroccan National Orchestra in an attempt to trace the origins of flamenco, connecting it with its Moorish past.

He began his career as a guitarist, but switched to singing at an early age, and he has evolved as one of the most innovative singers of flamenco. At an early age, he was strongly influenced by Antonio Mairena and Juan Talega, but would go on to develop his own unique vocal style.

During the 1960's and 70's, he was one of the top festival artistes, performing at many of the summer events that were held throughout Andalusia and the rest of Spain.

The recordings he made during the 1970's display his immense knowledge and expertise in the singing of the most orthodox styles of flamenco song.

He produced a unique record, *Persecution*, on which he traces the history and arrival of the Gypsies in Andalusia. The story is narrated by Felix Grande (flamencologist and author of *Memorias de Flamenco*) and tells of the many injustices committed against the Gypsies of Andalusia during the fifteenth century. The recording produces the ambience and feeling of the travelling Gypsy caravans, with typical songs such as tientos, siguiriyas and *caravanas*, accompanied by trundling wheels and the thumping of hooves.

The caravana is a style of cante of which his mother, La Perrata, was a master, and they are a style in which all the family would sing the chorus in harmony.

El Lebrijano has worked with some of the most illustrious names of the flamenco guitar, including Melchor de Marchena, Niño Ricardo, Manolo Sanlúcar, Juan Habichuela, and Paco de Lucía. With the latter, he recorded *El Lebrijano con la collaboration de Paco de Lucia*, an excellent example of El Lebrijano at his very best.

El Lebrijano still performs today, and his unique style of flamenco, mixed with Arabian and African music, has seen the stages in all corners of the world. He is considered one of the true pioneers of flamenco, because he has explored areas that had never before been ventured into in his search for the explanation of flamenco's roots.

This barely touches the surface of this most important flamenco dynasty, and although I have mentioned many great performers, to write a fully comprehensive work including dancers, guitarists and singers would require a work of many volumes.

Guitars and jaleos

I believe that many of best and most inspirational flamenco singers and dancers are those of Gypsy blood. However, this is not always the case with the guitar, because there have been many non-Gypsy, even non-Spanish, people who have mastered the instrument.

I am not suggesting that the flamenco guitar is an easy instrument to learn, on the contrary, because this clearly takes years of practice.

One of the most renowned flamenco guitarists, Paco de Lucía (who is not of Gypsy lineage), is considered to be one of the greatest Spanish guitarists of all time.

Francisco Sánchez Gómez - Paco de Lucía - has influenced more guitarists than anyone in the history of flamenco. He was born in Algeciras in 1947, and by the time he was seven, he was studying the guitar for around 12 hours a day. He has taken the guitar to new heights in flamenco, but to quote his own words, 'It's the voice first, and then the rhythm; all the rest comes after.'

It has only been in the last 30 years or so that the guitarist has been recognised on the covers of recordings. Prior to this, it was not felt to be of significant importance to include the guitarist's name on the credits. Paco de Lucía changed this, and he was the first guitarist to be credited on an album cover. He is listed on every disc by the late

Camarón de la Isla - a measure of his importance - and he has done more to promote the flamenco guitar both in Spain and worldwide than anyone else.

The flamenco guitar, like the Osborne Bull, is one of Spain's emblems, although it did not become an integral part of flamenco until the middle of the 19th century. No one can actually pinpoint the exact time at which it was introduced as an accompanying instrument, but it was the café cantante period that was largely responsible for the birth of the soloists.

It is of the utmost importance for an accompanist to know all the different styles of flamenco. It is the guitarist who follows the singer, and sometimes they might have had just a few minutes to discuss the style and key of the song they are about to perform together. However, most singers usually have a regular guitarist, someone they feel comfortable with, and someone who knows their capabilities. The guitarist needs good compás and has to stay out of the limelight, allowing the singer or dancer to shine rather than displaying his own talents.

The guitar is also used as a percussive instrument, giving the song a driving force of rhythm, especially with the technique known as the *rasgueado*, which is produced by heavily strumming the muted strings. Although this looks fairly easy to do, it is not, and only a good guitarist can produce the rhythms of a percussionist with ease. The guitarist will also use the face of the guitar, thumping out a rhythm with his thumb, the tips of his fingers, or the flat of his hand.

Many guitarists show their skills with the falsetas. These are guitar solos played at the beginning and the middle of the song. Some guitarists create their own falsetas, but the majority perform standards borrowed from guitarists of the past.

The flamenco guitar has very little in common with the classical guitar. Flamenco is more about expression, emotion, and driving rhythms, whereas the concert hall techniques of the classical guitarists are more concerned with crystal clear delivery. But the techniques used by today's flamenco soloists tend to be leaning more towards the classical guitar than the pure jondo style.

The jondo guitar has also been preserved, like the song, in certain towns and villages, and one important cradle for flamenco guitar is Morón de la Frontera. There, some of the most prominent guitarists, including Niño de Morón, Pepe Naranjo and Paco del Gastor, were born. This old flamenco town is perched high on a hill with panoramic views, especially the old part of the town, where the statue of the bald rooster keeps a vigilant eye.

The statue of the bronze rooster sits at the highest point of the town, close to the church of San Miguel and the ruins of the Roman castle. The legend of the bald rooster dates back to the fifteenth century and refers to a balding tax collector by the name of El Gallo, who was a fearful and merciless man who demanded much more in taxes from the poor farmers than was necessary. Demanding more and more money to feed his grand lifestyle, eventually the taxpayers had enough. On his next visit the fed-up residents of the town set upon him, and after a severe beating, he was covered with tar and stuck with feathers, then tied to his mule and sent packing, never to be seen in Morón de la Frontera again.

This rather ferocious looking rooster now watches over the countryside that surrounds Morón, and it is said to ward off any evil that may threaten the town.

There is a saying, '*Te vas a quedar como el gallo de Morón, sin plumas y cacareando en la mejor ocasión.*' This roughly translates as, 'Be careful, you'll end up like the rooster of Morón, bald and squawking.'

I was also told another amusing tale behind the legend of the rooster, although this one is based on an anecdote that dates back just to the civil war years. This amusing story was relayed to me by an Andalusian, and although I have no evidence that this event took place, it is a story that could well be true, so I include it anyway.

During the years of the civil war, many of the small towns, including Morón, were left in a state of poverty. The people had little or no money to buy food for their starving families and, in any case, there were times when there was simply no food to purchase. One day, a stray rooster wandered through the streets of Morón de la Frontera like a stranger in a western movie. Unaware that it was being watched, it pecked its way through the streets. Suddenly, in a moment of mayhem, a group of locals made a dash for the bird, which fled for its life with the hungry mob grabbing and snatching at it from behind. As dust and feathers from the progressively balding bird filled the air, the rooster took off squawking and flapping through the narrow streets.

But this rooster is not the town's only legend, as the steps that lead up to the Paseo el Gallo will demonstrate. On the wall at the top of these steps is a hand-painted plaque in memory of Diego Flores Amaya - Diego del Gastor.

This outstanding guitarist was born in Arriate, Málaga, but at an early age moved with his family to Gastor, the town from which he took his artistic name. He left Gastor when he was just ten years old and went to live in Morón de la Frontera, where his father had several businesses. He was Gypsy to the core, a man who treated the lower classes and outcasts with as much time and respect as anyone else, and he demanded that the Gypsies be treated in the same way.

Stories abound of Diego's eccentric ways, especially of how he had lost thousands of pesetas in lost earnings after storming out of paid juergas angered by a comment or action that he saw as derogatory to the Gypsy race.

There are a few DVDs available that show Diego accompanying some of flamenco's greatest singers, and if one watches this old footage, they will appreciate just what flamenco meant to him.

He was a favourite guitarist of La Fernanda and La Bernarda de Utrera, as well as Juan Talega, whom he accompanied on numerous occasions.

Diego played almost exclusively at private juergas in and around Morón de la Frontera. He was said to have been a shy man and that he avoided other famous guitarists, although he did agree to meet Sabicas. Sabicas, one of the most respected guitarists of his era, had travelled to Morón to see what all the fuss was about, for he had heard many stories of Diego's genius. During their meeting, Sabicas presented Diego with a Ramirez guitar, which Diego was reluctant to accept, because he was more comfortable playing his tatty old acoustic guitar. Diego's guitar was a means of expressing deep feeling, and it was not what he played, but how he played it. His creations were most often spontaneously invented in true flamenco fashion.

There have been many guitarists whose technical ability far exceeded Diego's antiquated style, but he played from the heart and each note was so meaningful. His style was simple, but simple only because he was not interested in showmanship or virtuosity.

He died in Morón on 7 July 1973, the very day he was to be honoured at the town's annual flamenco festival.

Diego del Gastor lived for the flamenco juerga lifestyle, enduring endless nights fuelled by the consumption of much alcohol, and he lived this life to the full. His doctor advised him to change his lifestyle, which would mean refraining from the flamenco 'way of life', advice he choose to ignore.

Morón has a couple of inviting old peñas, which are basically a social clubs. One is the *Peña Flamenca Montegil*. This peña was a little hard to find, and without the assistance of my guide that day, I would probably never have found it. My guide came in the shape of an aging man in a flat cap, with dry cracked skin that had been scorched by the many years he had spent working the land. Over a glass of wine and a cigarette (his fee for escorting me to the peña) we discussed Morón's flamenco heritage.

Most of the people in the bar were glued to a small television set that was showing an obviously important football match. In the corner, a group of stereotypical Andalusians were enjoying a game of dominoes, and even the loud bashing on the table or the slamming down of the last domino did not distract the others from their football.

This peña opened in 1992, and it displays many old photos of Diego performing with Juan Talega, La Fernanda de Utrera, and Antonio Mairena, during the town's annual flamenco festival- *El Gazpacho*.

I asked the barman, in my best Spanish, whether I could 'take a photograph', whilst pointing at the wall that was filled with old pictures. He looked in disbelief at my request and bluntly told me no! At first, I was confused at his refusal, but then realised that he thought I was asking for one of his. When I explained that I wanted permission to use my camera in the peña, he burst out laughing and said, '*hombre, of course.*'

As I stood revelling in the antiquated ambience of this peña, a fried sardine was placed in front of me, a free *tapa* to complement my glass of fino; along with an apology from the barmen. But it was me who needed to apologise, because my Spanish grammar is disgustingly bad for someone who has spent so many years in Spain: I should, by now, have a better understanding of the language!

One of Granada's most illustrious guitar dynasties is that of Habichuela, the patriarch of which was Tío José, born in 1909. He was a singer and guitarist who had an encyclopaedic knowledge of the styles from Sacromonte, although he was said to have excelled with the tangos. He avoided the commercial scene, preferring the intimate parties and family juergas. Of his many sons, the oldest and most well-known is Juan Habichuela, born in 1933. Juan began his career as a dancer, working alongside Mario Maya, but he later changed to the guitar. He played in many of the top tablaos in Madrid, accompanying Manolo Caracol, and later toured America with Fosforito. His son, Juan

Carmona - El Camborio – is a member of the flamenco fusion group, *Ketama*.

Augustín Castellón Campos – Sabicas - was another guitarist of great merit, although he spent the majority of his career outside Spain. It is said that Sabicas was responsible for promoting the flamenco guitar in the USA, a country in which he spent a great part of his life.

Born in Pamplona (Navarra) in 1912, he was just seven when he turned professional. By the age of ten, he was playing in some of the top clubs in Madrid.

This young Gypsy left Spain in 1937, after the outbreak of civil war, a time when he was romantically linked to the dancer Carmen Amaya. He spent twenty years living in Mexico, and in 1957, he went to America, never to return to live in his native Spain.

Sabicas was described as the greatest flamenco guitarist in the world. He recorded many discs as a solo artiste, and he was no stranger to accompanying the dance and song. He recorded with Camarón de la Isla, El Sordera, and Enrique Morente, to name a few.

Sabicas was considered a genius, and his contribution to the art of flamenco has been a milestone in the evolution of the flamenco guitar. There are certain techniques which Sabicas created that are still used by today's guitarists, and these are considered to be essential to achieve the 'flamenco sound'.

He died in New York in 1990.

One of my favourite guitarists is Manuel Moreno Junquera, or Moraito Chico, as he is known. Moraito was born into the heart of Jerez's Gypsy flamenco, and within his family are some of the most illustrious names in the history of the art. He is the son of Juan Morao, and nephew of Manuel Morao, two of the most renowned and respected guitarists in Jerez. Manuel Morao was the founder of *Gitanos de Jerez*, an organisation that promotes and helps up-and-coming Gypsy artistes from Jerez de la Frontera.

Moraito started his career playing in the tablao *Los Canasteros* in Madrid, but his biggest break came when he began accompanying La Paquera de Jerez. Today he is one of the most sought-after accompanists, and he has become the preferred guitarist of José Mercé.

José Fernandez Torres, or Tomatito, is the guitarist who took over from Paco de Lucía as the accompanist of Camarón de la Isla. Born in 1958 in Almería, he has, since the death of Camarón, dedicated his art to the solo flamenco guitar. He is a prolific guitarist, but like Vicente Amigo and Paco de Lucía, he is now fusing flamenco with many different styles of music.

A DVD that demonstrates the chemistry between Tomatito and Camarón is *Camarón-Paris 87/88*. It was recorded when Camaron's health was rapidly declining, although it worth watching just to see their hairstyles.

I never had the privilege of seeing Tomatito assist Camarón de la Isla in concert, but I did see him perform solo in the bullring in Málaga. Unfortunately, on that night, gone was the jondo style of guitar that he produced for Camarón.

Though not wishing to upset any flamenco guitarists, I always feel that something is missing from a solo guitar recital: the voice. Flamenco can be appreciated without the dance, and it can be appreciated without the guitar, but without the voice, the guitar becomes something different. The role of the guitar in flamenco was originally a rhythmic accompaniment to give the song an organised structure and a driving force. The flamenco guitar differs from the classical guitar in the instrument itself, and in the technique used to play it. Today, however, the solo flamenco guitarist uses techniques from the classical school and, in this way, it has become a separate art of its own. Many have entered into areas that are not considered to be conventional

Guitarists such as Sabicas were responsible for the promotion of the solo flamenco guitar around the world, and scores of others have carved lucrative careers by becoming virtuosos of the solo instrument.

The soloist, as with the accompanist, will spend up to ten hours a day practising, and his guitar literally becomes an extension of his arms.

The accompanist learns his art by enduring many hours of juerga, where he will learn the song styles so well that he will almost be able to sing them himself.

Most people who have an interest in jondo flamenco will agree that the most important part of the song is its words, especially the way singer interprets them. There will be those who disagree, and it will depend on one's personal taste. Many foreigners prefer the mellow sound of the guitar, compared to the echo gitano most suited to cante jondo.

The cante is probably the most difficult to appreciate or understand, and is too often written off as just an unbearable mass of noise that has no tune or melody.

In the flamenco tablaos, it is most commonly the dancers that the audience is there to see, and anything the singer is doing will often be of no importance to them. Even if they have no idea about flamenco, they can appreciate the grace and passion of the dancer, and this also can be said of the solo flamenco guitar.

Many previous non-Spanish writers have been guitarists who have come to Andalusia to study flamenco. I am not a guitarist; if I was, maybe it would have been a little easier to understand and appreciate flamenco when I first became interested. For me, however, it was a case of slow discovery and searching, without the benefit of being able to accompany the artistes, other than with the palmas and jaleo. Having said this, to get involved in any way is a wonderful experience, no matter what part you play.

Jaleo basically means 'hell raising', or 'encouragement'. In whatever way it presents itself, the jaleo is practised by anyone who is present.

Jaleo is a very exciting part of flamenco, because everyone supports the singer or dancer, showing his or her emotional approval and encouraging the performer to find the duende. Listening to the recordings of the older singers, this is emphasised very much.

One night, in a popular flamenco tavern in Seville, while watching a singer perform some very moving and heartfelt songs, I noticed a party of British people, and judging by their reaction, it was their first encounter with orthodox flamenco. Shouts of encouragement from the audience filled the room. These cries show respect and approval, and spur the artiste to even greater heights. However, all in the British party were horrified at the outburst, finding such behaviour rude and offensive. As with most people who are not familiar with the art of flamenco, especially the British - taught only ever watch in silence, providing polite applause between songs - this loud, raucous aspect of flamenco can be distressing. Many of the early artistes who visited Britain commented on how different the audiences were compared to those in Spain.

Flamenco is not just song, dance or guitar, but a collection of components that go together to make this phenomenon, and without the jaleo it would be like a football match without the crowd.

Watching good *palmeros* perform is a pleasure on its own. The rhythms they play can be very complex and are difficult to master. It certainly isn't just 'clapping along'; it takes practice and stamina, as the mercifully brief, stuttered, off-rhythm slaps of those who insist on doing it badly shows.

Many of the tablao dance shows focus on the footwork – zapateado - and this will be accompanied by the intricate counter-rhythms of the palmeros, which will be ringing in one's ears long after they have left the show.

Another instrument now widely used in flamenco is the *cajón*. This is a wooden box-drum on which the percussionist sits. In the back of the box is a hole, roughly the size of that found on an acoustic guitar, with a hinged paddle to control the tone. Several thin wires are secured to the inside of the front panel. The sounds produced depend on where it is struck. It has a deep bass drum sound if struck in the middle, and a sharp snare drum sound when hit near the top.

Fandangos and malagueñas

I had no idea what was in store for me when I first began to work on this book, for I did not realise that this project would take me on a journey to many different towns and villages in search of the mysteries and legends of this art. I have travelled through many of Andalusia's most quaint and picturesque settings, as well as large cities like Seville and Cádiz, and I came to realise just how much importance individual towns and villages had on the style of the flamenco they produced. This became even more evident when wandering around the antiquated back streets of the neighbourhood of Santiago in Jerez de la Frontera. Time seems to have stood still in some of these dusty old towns. These predominately Gypsy districts still produce an orthodox style of flamenco singing that is fast disappearing from other regions. There are always exceptions, but other than Utrera, Lebrija and Jerez de la Frontera, which are still producing artistes of the more traditional styles, many of the old areas associated with flamenco seem to have been left along the way.

Málaga, however, has adhered to a flamenco tradition that has often been overlooked by past writers of the subject. Unfortunately, for the past forty years, Málaga has become better known for its cheap package holidays rather than its flamenco.

It is true that Málaga has not produced the amount of legendary flamenco artistes that Jerez de la Frontera has, but it is still producing its own unique style of flamenco, based around the fandangos.

There have been some very important artistes who put Málaga on the flamenco map, such as Juan Breva, La Trini, La Repompa and El Piyayo. Today's singers include Bonela Hijo, Andres Lozano, La Cañeta and Rocío Bázan, who are accompanied by equally competent guitarists like El Chaparro, Antonio Soto, Curro de Maria and Andres Cansino.

There are also many good dancers such as Rocío Molina and El Carrete, to name just two. One of the most promising dancers from this province is Sergío Aranda, a youngster who is fast becoming one of the best bailaores that Málaga has produced for many years.

Sergio Aranda excels in the styles of the bulerías, seguidilla and the bambera, during which, he teases the audience with his jacket like a bullfighter teases a bull with his cape. He has an impeccable sense of rhythm and an incredible knowledge of most flamenco styles. His strutting routines are sharp and exciting, and his dance is old school with a touch of young magic. Sergio Aranda is for sure one of the most aspiring young flamenco dancers to appear from Málaga for some time and he is proof that Málaga is producing some extremely good young flamenco artistes.

The roots of Málaga's flamenco tradition seem to lie with its most famous contributor, Juan Breva. Breva was a singer and guitarist responsible for popularising the malagueña, a style of fandango favoured by non-gypsy singers of his era. He became the highest paid singer, earning 25 pesetas a show, and he was said to have regularly made as many as three performances a night at different café cantantes in Madrid. He became rich and relatively famous in an extremely short period of time.

Born Antonio Ortega Escalona, in Vélez Málaga in 1844, he acquired the name Breva because he sold figs (brevas) as a child with his grandfather in the streets of Vélez-Málaga.

Most singers of this era sang only for pleasure, among a close-knit circle of friends, and payment was simply the appreciation they were shown. Breva, who was partially blind, sang a form of malagueña that was derived from the verdiales, and he wrote most of his own lyrics, something that was quite unusual at that time.

This new, 'polished' style of flamenco soon caught the attention of the general public and catapulted Breva to stardom. He took the malagueña to such heights that he became the most popular singer in the cafés, but unbeknown to him, he was about to start the decline of cante jondo.

The malagueñas swept across Andalusia, and, at one time, there were more one-cante specialists of the malagueña than any other style.

Suddenly the gachos had an idol of the masses. Until then, the majority of good flamenco performers were Gypsies who sang styles of song from the western areas of Andalusia, but Juan Breva was about to change all of this.

He was the first flamenco singer to perform at the royal palace, singing for King Alfonso XII and Queen María Cristina. Breva, who was crowned 'king of the malagueñas', became a regular performer at the palace and he is said to have obtained a large collection of gold tiepins given to him as gifts by King Alfonso.

Despite his fame and fortune, he died in poverty, and legend claims that a collection was held by fellow colleagues to pay for his funeral.

The malagueñas became popular with many singers outside Málaga, and also with Gypsies, including Enrique el Mellizo, who created his own distinctive styles. Today, the malagueña is very much part of the flamenco repertoire, although it has been far removed from the versions that Juan Breva sang.

At the beginning of the twentieth century, there were eleven café cantantes in Málaga, one of which was *El Café del Sevillano*, later to become *El Café Suizo,* an establishment favoured by Don Antonio Chacón. It was in this café that the renowned guitarist Niño de Lucena is said to have entered into a competition playing the guitar wearing gloves, yet performing his falsetas with absolute perfection. Why, remains a mystery.

Malaga was also home to *El Café El Chinitas*, an establishment that has gone down in flamenco history, because some of the greatest singers of the late 19th and early 20th century performed at this venue, including Don Antonio Chacón, La Argentinita and, of course, Juan Breva. The site of the old theatre, which is in Pasaje El Chinitas (off Calle Larios), has been marked by a ceramic plaque that also records that it was a favourite haunt of poet Federico García Lorca.

The café, which took its name from an actor, opened in 1860 and became the most famous of its kind in Málaga. The establishment changed its name to the *Salon Royal* when flamenco started its decline, and it became more of a cabaret club. Most singing cafes had disappeared by 1920, but the *Salon Royal* survived until 1941.

The building that housed the café is now a material shop and the only reminder of its glory days is a ceramic plaque high on the wall above the door, which celebrates the fiftieth anniversary of Federico García Lorca's death. García Lorca was a regular visitor to the café and he immortalised it in one of his poems.

Not far from the original *Café de Chinitas*, in Calle Moreno Monroy, one will find El Meson de Chinitas, which, as its name might suggest, offers a genuine flamenco ambience. The exterior displays interesting ceramics with poems referring to Malaga's flamenco tradition, especially what Machado termed 'Malaga Cantaora'; while the interior walls are decorated with paintings and photographs of some of Málaga's finest artistes, such as

El Principe Gitano, Miguel de los Reyes, La Paula and Chiquito de la Calzada.

Now a house-hold name on television, Chiquito de la Calzada (1932), began his career as a flamenco singer who regularly performed in the *Bodegas El Pimpi* in Málaga. He went on to perform in Madrid, returning to Málaga to work in the *Tablao El Jaleo* in Torremolinos.

Another bar that played its part in Malaga's flamenco legacy was *La Taverna Gitana*, which was the bar where a very young Camarón de la Isla made one of his first professional appearances: years later, it would also be the place where he would first meet the guitarist Tomatito. This bar was later converted into the *Tablao Torres Bermejas*, which, in the 1960s and '70s, was among the most popular flamenco haunts in the city.

One of the old flamenco centres in Málaga is the district of El Perchel. This area is no longer tied to much flamenco activity, but is remembered for the many flamenco artistes that were born there.

One legendary singer, famed for his tangos, was Rafael Flores Nieto, El Piyayo, who was born in Málaga in 1864. It is said that El Piyayo was the innovator of the *tango de Málaga*, which was a name attributed by Antonio Mairena. El Piyayo spent his childhood in Cuba, during the War of Independence, and it was from here that he developed his distinctive Latin-style tangos.

El Piyayo is remembered in Málaga as someone who rarely worked, but who spent his days sleeping, and his nights wandering the streets of El Perchel singing tangos. He was no stranger to the jailhouse in Málaga, as his nights of hellraising and drunkenness would often end there.

He cut a somewhat ghostly character, with shoddy clothes that hung from his spindly body, rendering him worthy of his nickname of El Piyayo - 'the little rogue'.

La Repompa, who was born in El Perchel in 1937, was said to have been an excellent interpreter of the tientos, bulerías, and rumbas, sheshe was best known for her style of tangos, which she learnt from La Pirula, another of the district's renowned singers.

La Repompa was a regular performer at the now demolished tablao El Refugio in Málaga, although she headed to Seville to work with Pastora Imperio, which is when she began receiving recognition.

In 1959, she was invited to sing at El Pardo in front of Franco, but her appearance had to be cancelled due to ill health. She returned to Málaga, where she died of peritonitis eight days later. She left an impeccable stamp on the flamenco history of Málaga, and members of her family, which includes her sister, La Repompilla, are still at the forefront of the flamenco scene.

Teresa Sánchez Campos, known as La Cañeta de Málaga, is another member of this family. Daughter of La Pirula, she was born in El

Perchel circa 1940, although her exact date of birth is something of a mystery. She began her commercial career in Madrid in 1960, and went on to travel the world with renowned dancer Antonio Gades.

She was also part of the flamenco group, Los Vargas, which included several local flamenco luminaries, although today, she usually performs with her husband, singer Jose Sálazar.

La Cañeta is one of Malaga's most radiant flamenco performers, a dynamic fiestera whose bulerias are lively, exciting and full of Gypsy personality. Today, her voice is full of a fierce and burning passion, evidence that Málaga still has some truly worthwhile artistes.

Another of the great artistes to be associated with Malaga (even though he was born in Córdoba) is the veteran singer, Fosforito, who was justly awarded the fifth golden key of flamenco during Malaga's first flamenco biennial festival in 2005.

Antonio Fernandez Diaz, Fosforito, was born in Puente Genil in 1932, but has lived in the province of Málaga for many years. He is considered one of the most important singers of the 20th century, and this becomes obvious watching him perform live.

Fosforito excels in the most ancient and authentic style of flamenco, 'a golpe', a style that's rhythm is supplied by the singer's knuckles on the table top. His encyclopaedic knowledge of flamenco song has made him one of the basic pillars of the natural school of flamenco. He combines this vast amount of knowledge with his rigorous sense of rhythm in order to reproduce song styles that are rarely sung by other singers. He has revived forgotten styles like the zángano from Puente Genil, and brought new life to countless other old forms of flamenco song.

He began singing at local fairs, cattle markets and brothels, but his career took off in 1956, when he won every prize in the non-professional section of the Córdoba Concurso de Cante Jondo.

His early influences came from singers like Tomás and Pastora Pavón, Pepe Pinto, Juan Valdarrama and Enrique Montoya, but his singing career nearly ended before it had begun. In 1955, after a stomach operation, he lost his voice and it looked as though he might never sing again. He returned to Puente Genil disappointed and distressed at the thought of a future without being able to sing. Puente Genil town hall came to his rescue and brought him a Santos Hernández guitar, and arranged for him to have lessons, but Fosforito knew that it was the singing of flamenco that really interested him. On the eve of the *Córdoba Concurso de Cante Jondo*, Fosforito decided to try his luck at singing again, as his voice had started to return to its previous strength, and also because he was desperately short of money. He was a revelation, winning first prize in all categories, which included difficult styles like the polo, caña, soleá and serrana.

After his success in Cordoba, Fosforito headed to the capital to perform at the Teatro de la Zarzuela with the dancer Mariemma, and from here, he was employed at the Madrid tablao El Corral de la Moreria.

He went on to perform at most of the top flamenco tablaos and appeared at many of the flamenco festivals in Andalusia, sharing the bill with artistes like Antonio Mairena, a life-long friend.

In 1962, he competed in the third Llave de Oro del Cante competition in Córdoba, although the award went to his friend Mairena. As one writer at the time declared, 'Whilst the key went to Antonio Mairena, it was Fosforito who helped forge the lock into which it fits.'

Fosforito has had a most brilliant career that has seen many awards and much praise bestowed upon him. In 1968, the Cátedra de Flamencologia de Jerez de la Frontera (professorship of flamencology) honoured him with the national prize for cante; and in 1985, he was awarded the second Compás del Cante. In 1999, he was presented with the coveted Premio Pastora Pavón, the highest flamenco award given by the Junta de Andalucía (regional government).

His home town of Puente Genil has, since 1967, dedicated its flamenco festival to Fosforito, and as well as making him the town's Hijo Predilecto (favourite son): it has also given him the Medalla de Oro de Puente Genil.

Fosforito has twelve flamenco peñas named after him in Spain, one of which is in Málaga. He has to his credit more than thirty recordings, one of which is the vast *Antológica del Cante Flamenco*, which he recorded with Paco de Lucía in 1969. The anthology contains forty-eight different song styles and demonstrates his vast instruction of some of the most antiquated flamenco styles, including soleá apolá, verdiales, malagueña de La Trini, caña and polo, and a saeta antígua de Puente Genil.

Fosforito is not a Gypsy and he does not have the voz afillá that is normally associated with them, but he does have an exceptional depth and range.

He writes his own lyrics, something rarely done by flamenco singers, and composes songs for other flamenco artistes, which in the past has included Camarón de la Isla.

The highlight of Fosforito's career came in 2005 when he was awarded the fifth *Llave de Oro* in Málaga, forty-three years after he had competed for the third golden key back in 1962. Fosforito is blessed with the gift that allows flamenco to express all of life's emotions, a gift that is bestowed on only a few of the true masters of this art.

He can still be seen performing at peñas and festivals, although today he is more selective as to where he performs, unlike his youth when he would sing anywhere just to put food on the table.

On one occasion, during the Málaga biennial, I was fortunate enough to see Fosforito perform in the *Castillo el Bil Bil*, in Benalmádena Costa, although there was some confusion as to whether the general public would be allowed entry, as most of the seats were reserved for the bigwigs of the town hall. As I was being informed that there were no seats available, I noticed that Fosforito and his guitarist, Antonio Soto, had slipped into a small adjoining bar for a quick refreshment before the performance, so I decided to approach them to see if I could gain entry. I explained that I was a writer and that I was working on a book about flamenco, but mostly, that I was an avid fan of his and wanted so much to see tonight's show.

Ten minutes later, after Fosforito saw to it that I was allowed entry, I found myself sat in the front row of the small patio where he was to perform. It was a very intimate setting with only about fifty invited guests, with whom Fosforito mingled and chatted, looking very relaxed and at ease. He gave a lecture before the show, in which he discussed the evolution of flamenco singing, as he is one of the leading authorities on this subject.

The night was special because it was very intimate, and Fosforito was in fine form, chatting and laughing with the small audience. After the show, I watched as he signed autographs, posed for photographs and generally related to his fans; nothing seemed too much trouble for him. He is truly one of the gentlemen of flamenco.

One will also find some old bars and peñas in Málaga that have contributed to the flamenco history of the city, and one in particular can be found close to the new Picasso Museum in Calle Granada.

The bodega *El Pimpi* is something of an institution for flamenco in Malaga; its old walls hold many memories of some of the finest artistes that have performed there over the years. This is the one place in Málaga where one will witness the most orthodox styles of this art, no frills or expensive niceties, just cante, wine, and a little piece of flamenco history.

The walls of this old establishment are plastered with old posters advertising bullfights and ferias from an Andalusia of years past. The wall that runs the length of the bar is covered with photographs of the many celebrities and personalities that have visited the bar in its long history. The main area is lined with the large oak barrels that hold gallons of Málaga's renowned *vinos dulces*, each of which has a message or drawing scribbled by artistes who have passed through it.

One night I remember with great fondness happened during a performance that was to be staged on the outside patio in June. It was a beautiful, jasmine-perfumed setting, just yards from the Roman amphitheatre. However, the singer, Antoñita Contreras, probably performed a set far superior and intimate than the one she had prepared for.

As we sat waiting for the show to begin, the unimaginable happened - it started to rain. Everyone ran to shelter under the nearby trees to wait for the downpour to stop, but this had obviously set in for the night. As this show was to be held outside, instead of in the bodega, there were nearly twice the usual number of people attending. One would have imagined that the show would be cancelled, as it would be impossible to fit everyone inside. I decided to head for the bar for a consolation drink, bitterly disappointed that the show would be cancelled. Suddenly I heard the faint tones of cante coming from the interior of the bodega. There were no microphones for either singer or guitarist: they were simply getting drenched outside. The people had crammed in and were standing on chairs, beer crates, or whatever they could clamber upon to see what was happening. The audience, although a little uncomfortable, cheered and encouraged this impromptu performance, which lasted just 20 minutes due to the intense heat created by the mass of bodies.

Some of my most memorable nights of flamenco have occurred in *El Pimpi*. There have been many times while writing this book that I have found it difficult to fully describe the feeling and ambience created in these delightful old bars. This is something one must experience for themselves.

Another memorable night occurred during the city's *Semana Santa* celebrations. Veteran singer Antonio de Canillas entertained with some excellently performed saetas, and this was one of the only times that I had experienced a silenced audience. Normally, this bar is filled with riotous jaleo, but on this night, the audience hung on his every word.

Virgins, processions and pilgrimages

Every province of Andalusia, including the smallest towns and villages, come out in force for the week of *Semana Santa*. Roads are shut off, public transport is thrown into chaos, and the shortest of journeys will take forever to complete. Banks and shops close, and the streets are filled with hundreds of thousands of people who flock to watch the scenes of the Passion that are paraded through the streets, morning, noon, and night.

Some of the processions do not start until around 2am, then continue for around 12 hours, before returning to the church from which they had started. The pasos, as they are called in Seville, or tronos, in Málaga, are carried by up to two hundred people who, for weeks after Easter, are still suffering from excruciating back and neck pains.

The floats are owned by Lay Confraternities, whose job it is to organise the itinerary for the week's processions, and they are also responsible for the upkeep of the images.

There has been a long running altercation between the people of Seville and those of Málaga as to whose Semana Santa celebrations are the best. Malagueños accuse the Sevillians of being supercilious. The people of Seville will dismiss the importance of Easter in Málaga, as many believe that their floats, and in particular, the way they are carried, are far superior to those of Málaga.

In Málaga, the floats are huge, whereas in Seville they are smaller, yet no less stunning, to enable them to be manoeuvred through the tiny cobbled streets.

I must admit that what I have experienced in Seville has been far more moving than what I have seen in Málaga, although I have attended Seville's Easter festivities many more times than Malaga's.

The emotion stirred during these incense-drenched processions is ecstatic. Women clutch at their rosaries and mutter prayers, although many of them will have rarely seen the inside of a church the rest of the year.

The Gypsy processions in both Seville and Málaga are quite a spectacle, as these are more joyous and colourful, because they dance and sing bulerías to the images as they pass. Their processions have the feel of a Gospel service, as opposed to the typically devout Catholic ordeals.

The gitanos, who refer to Jesus as Senór Manuel, celebrate in true Gypsy demeanour, and their disregard for rules and regulations is evident even during Holy Week. The pasos have a certain route and timetable to adhere to, but the Gypsies are normally too busy enjoying the procedure to worry about a planned schedule, resulting in the confraternities being fined for not adhering to the time allowed for the route.

Obviously, the processions in the cities are far bigger and more elaborate than those in the smaller towns and villages, but most often one will have a better idea of what's going on in these smaller parades.

I remember my first encounter with the Easter celebrations, which happened in one of the small towns just outside Málaga. My first impression of the *nazareno* was, I must admit, a rather anxious experience. The hooded spectacles, which are alarmingly reminiscent of the Ku Klux Klan, headed in our direction, wooden cross and burning candles at the front of the procession. The sheer size of the heavily decorated floats was awe-inspiring. The smell of incense fused with the aroma of jasmine mingled in the warm evening air, and the eerie tone of the bell being struck as the pasos approached added a primeval ambience.

I once came so close to a paso in Seville, I had to inhale deeply as it passed. Hundreds of people had lined Calle Franco waiting patiently for the procession of Christo de Burgos to appear. The nazarenos appeared first, dressed in dark blue hoods, with white robes and hessian cummerbunds, carrying dripping white candles. Some of the nazarenos were blindfolded or barefoot, done as an act of penance for their sins.

It was a silent procession, no loud marching band, just the occasional call from the lead man whose job it was to guide the costaleros along the narrow street. People were forced to stand with their backs pressed tightly against the shop window as the huge religious image was slowly shuffled passed. Adrenalin was sent rushing through my body as I realised the sheer weight and size of this huge float, as it passed just a few centimetres from my face.

When the virgin approached, we were instructed to move, as this float was even larger. Tradition declares that one must not turn their back on the Virgin, so I, and hordes of other spectators, was forced to walk backwards with this giant platform heading in my direction. Some people began to panic in the rush to get out of the way, which is not the best situation to be in when you are walking backwards at quite a pace along with hundreds of other people.

Easter is one of the most magical times to visit Andalusia, because it demonstrates the utterly baroque nature of its traditions and its people. Hundreds of thousands of people, more than for any other occasion, come together for a week of religious worship.

During the daytime, the women traditionally dress in black with lace shawls and a peineta, or hair comb, which sits high on her head. The size or height of the peineta depends on the time of day that it is worn. This is complemented with a long lace trail that is clipped in position down her back.

The images can be visited in the church when they are not embarking on their journey, and this is when people file past, kissing them and offering a prayer of hope or forgiveness. Whether catholic or not, one cannot help but be moved by the life-like scenes of the last week of Jesus Christ's life.

Another curious spectacle to happen during Easter week is the singing of the saeta, during which, the singer will show his devotion to a particular image of Christ or the Virgin. To witness an ancient saeta performed from a balcony in a narrow, darkened street is an experience that will leave most people drained of emotion.

Although saetas are now part of many flamenco singers' repertoires, the most emotionally inspiring ones are encountered in the early hours of the morning in somewhere like Triana.

Manuel Vallejo and Pastora Pavón were two of the most sought-after singers of the saeta during Holy Week in Seville during the mid-1920s.

Manuel Torre was also an excellent interpreter of them: it is said that he once sang a two-hour saeta to the Virgin de la Macarena, bringing the centre of Seville to a grinding halt. Today, the pasos are only allowed to stop for two or three minutes for the saeta to be performed.

The saeta, which comes from the Latin word *sagitta* (arrow). is not flamenco in origin, although it has all the spontaneity of flamenco because it is sung by anyone who feels moved by the occasion. Most often, today, they are organised and sung by professional singers at pre-planned points along the route. Obviously, they lose their spontaneity and feeling when rehearsed. Much better is the genuine emotional outburst from someone moved by the proceedings, as the sound of this ancient cry can be a most emotive experience.

The saeta has all the primitive tones of the debla or martinet, and like many flamenco styles, there are various theories as to its origins. It is believed to have become popular around 1840, although its roots can be traced back further than this. It is of common belief, although never proven, that it evolves from Jewish religious songs.

Semana Santa has little to do with flamenco other than the saeta, but in the minds of many, it also has little to do with religion either.

It is of common belief that it is more a chance for the Andalusians to dress up, parade the streets and do what it would appear they like doing most, enjoying a fiesta.

This is also evident during the romerias, or pilgrimages, which take place in several locations in Andalusia throughout the year.

Torremolinos (Malaga) hosts the second largest pilgrimage in Andalucía after El Rocío, held in Huelva each May.
The event, which takes place on the third Sunday of September, attracts not only the locals of the Costa del Sol town, but pilgrims from all over the region. The festivities, which honour the town's patron, Archangel San Miguel, attract around 200,000 people, who dance and sang behind a procession of oxen drawn floats that wind their way through the streets of the town and on to the El Pinar woods. Here, they embark on

an afternoon of frivolous fun, followed by a mass in honour of the patron at the small shrine located on the outskirts of the town.

This event, declared a Festival of National Tourist Interest, is dripping in Andalusian custom and tradition, and along with the brightly decorated carts, the day offers an insight into a typical celebration. The women wear colourful flamenco-style dresses, while the men are attired in cordovan hats and rociero clothing for a day that offers a post-card image of a truly Spanish festivity.

Although this pilgrimage, which signals the start of the town's fair, now attracts thousands of visitors, it began as a fairly modest gathering, although no one seems certain of the year it first appeared.

According to local author José Lacuey, this pilgrimage, a pagan-religious festival, 'dates back to very ancient times, so old that it is lost in history'.

Although verbal tradition affirms that the event was already celebrated before the 1930s, the first information about the pilgrimage is from 1940.

The Malaga author, Carlos Blanco, refutes that it was established prior to 1930. Blanco used feria programmes from 1917, and from 1926 until 1929 for his research, and he claims that there is 'no documented evidence' that it began to be celebrated before the Civil War (1936-39). He goes on to say that newspapers of that time, such as El Regional, usually reported on the Torremolinos fair, but during these years there was no reference to a pilgrimage.

Blanco states that the first certified evidence of this pilgrimage dates to 1940. He bases his findings on a article published in a Malaga newspaper on 29 September 1940, which reported that the people of Torremolinos were summoned to a 'great pilgrimage'.

Although no one seems to know why, the popularity of the romeria faded during the 1960s, and did not regain its vigour until the 1970s.

In 1972, just four floats were followed by around 200 people; while in 1977, there were five times as many floats and more than 20,000 pilgrims.

In the first years of the 21st century, the gathering reached unprecedented popularity, with a massive influx of more than a quarter of a million people, leading to headlines claiming that Torremolinos romeria is the second most popular after that of El Rocío.

I have attended the romería in Torremolinos on many occasions, and each year I am overcome by the wonderful atmosphere and the friendliness of the people. Local breweries set up makeshift bars selling beer, and paella, which is made in giant paella pans that measure about two metres in diameter.

In the alleyways and plazas, in fact, anywhere that it is possible, along the route, singing, dancing, and merrymaking fills the air.

Many of the revellers bring their own food and drink, and the whole family will stake their claim to a plot of land in the woods, where they will enjoy the celebration for the entire day. The smell of sardines cooked on barbecues mingles with the pine-tinted air, while thousands of people party in typical Andalusian style.

On one occasion, my group of friends, which, consisted of around ten people, had claimed their plot of land, and blankets were spread out on the floor, along with the iceboxes, which contained food and wine to help us through the long day.

Opposite our plot was another party of Spanish revellers that had in their company a collection of American tourists who seemed to be overwhelmed by what they saw.

Loud sevillana music bellowed from the floats and carts that were still arriving at the pinewoods, while the huge bulls and donkeys, which were tied to trees, seemed oblivious to the goings on as children petted and fussed them.

The bar areas were packed to the limits as people tussled for an opening in which they could attract the barmen's attention.

The party opposite ours was starting to warm up to the sound of sevillanas and light flamenco. One of the revellers was sat astride a cajón pounding out a rhythm, which enticed the four gaily-dressed woman to dance, swirling their arms and dresses in motion to the thumping rhythms.

We decided to join in with shouts of approval and much hand clapping, and soon one of our group was up dancing with them. As he is from Seville, he wanted to dance a sevillana, and he instructed me to join him on the cajón, much to the surprise and intrigue of the Spanish. 'An Englishman on the cajón, does he know the rhythms?'

The Americans seemed pleased that we had joined in their celebrations, as they were experiencing communication problems, but nobody was concerned, because the real communication was the riotous clapping and foot stomping that accompanied the dancer.

One of the Americans explained that this was her first time in Europe, claiming that what she had experienced during this romería was one of the most exciting parts of her trip.

One of the group produced a frying pan that only a short while before was being used to cook chorizo and blood sausage, which he used as a *tinaja* with great results. A tinaja is a ceramic percussion instrument used in Arabic and African music, and this frying pan proved to be an excellent substitute.

As I thumped away on the cajón, I noticed that we were surrounded by others who had come over to join in the fun. Wine and cigarettes were being exchanged, and as soon as one song stopped, someone would engage with the clapping once more, encouraging everyone to continue, with barely the time to catch their breath.

We played, sang and danced until the night came, everyone living life to the full for a few hours, not a care in the world other than enjoying music and dance in the juerga style.

I never knowingly met any of those people again, but for that fiesta we were the best of friends.

This pilgrimage is one of the biggest in Spain, and just to be part of it, whether you are simply a spectator, or actively involved, is an experience that will take some beating.

I was once asked what it is about Andalusia that I find so attractive, and the answer is simple. Since I became involved with flamenco, I have been introduced to so many aspects of Spanish life that I had previously not experienced. Andalusia has brought something out of me that I didn't know existed: what I love the most is the person it has made me.

Tablaos and peñas

The tablaos are basically modern-day cafés cantantes. They are the commercial flamenco clubs that were chiefly aimed at foreign visitors, especially in tourist areas like the Costa del Sol. If it's pure, undiluted flamenco that one is in search of, it won't normally be found in the tablaos.

The arrival of tourism, which was to help lift Spain, especially Andalusia, out of its almost third-world status, destroyed the greater part of the coastline of southern Spain. The tranquil fishing villages that were dotted along the Mediterranean coast were transformed into concrete tourist havens. Every available piece of land became a construction site in order to accommodate the thousands of tourists who flocked to the coast of the sun, although few of them were familiar with Andalusian traditions or culture

The tablaos started to spring up all over Andalusia, but, unfortunately, many of them offered a flamenco that is a far cry from the real thing. The cante is often weak or absent altogether, and a more choreographed style of flamenco dance is offered to the tourists, who are usually the tablaos' main source of income.

Sexy young maidens with their colourful dresses and castanets were offered in place of the real Gypsy beauties, as it was obvious that the average customer would not appreciate the true form of this art.

Tablao flamenco is often inferior: the dance routines are performed the same each night, and even the dancers can seem bored with it all. The majority of these clubs promote good-looking girls in frilly dresses who just go through the motions, often with no drive or motivation, only choreographed passionless dance. Add to this the extortionate entrance fee, and the fact that you may even be dragged from your seat and hideously embarrassed up on the stage, and it doesn't conjure the most authentic setting for flamenco.

Images of Andalusian beauties wearing colourful flamenco dresses, along with the emblematic flamenco guitar and rattling castanets, are portrayed in tourist propaganda and the media. In Seville, one is constantly reminded of the province's connection with flamenco, especially in areas like Santa Cruz and El Arenal. Souvenir and gift shops will tempt visitors with an array of cheap and tacky flamenco dolls, posters and dresses.

The majority of Seville's tablaos are located in the old district, but the quality of the flamenco will vary from over-theatrical and over-rehearsed, to a few higher-standard clubs. The best of Seville's flamenco will be found in the bars and taverns, but for the tourists, the tablaos are hard to ignore. On street corners and in souvenir shops, posters advertising 'The most authentic Andalusian art', or, 'The best flamenco in Seville', will be found in abundance

Unfortunately, the extortionate entrance fees and price of the drinks is normally enough to convince the unsuspecting tourist that they are witnessing a pure and ancient art.

But it's not all over-priced glitter-flamenco in Seville, because there are a few tablaos that offer a more genuine insight into the real thing and even though they are still expensive, they are better than the average tourist claptraps, of which there are plenty.

El Patio Sevillano is one of Seville's most famous tablaos, but not necessarily one of its best. Founded in 1952, it is advertised as 'authentic flamenco performed by the best artistes', but this tablao is a mixture of classic Spanish dance, and flamenco, so it offers more of a cabaret-style ambience than a pure flamenco one.

In the Santa Cruz district of the city, one will find the tablao *El Gallo,* which has been in existence since 1966, and has helped many of today's artistes on their way to stardom.

Cristina Hoyos, Matilda Coral, Antonio Mairena, and El Farruco all passed through this tablao's doors in the early stages of their careers.

El Gallo is situated in a picturesque plaza huddled between 18th century buildings in the heart of the Barrio de Santa Cruz. It is a small, intimate tablao with elegant decoration, with the exception of the rather tacky stage area, but it does offer some decent flamenco.

The district of El Arenal offers a few tablaos, but more appealing for those that enjoy spontaneous flamenco outbursts will be the bars in

Calle Arfe. A few of the bars in this street are renowned for their afternoon party sessions, which attract flamenco aficionados and, on occasion, celebrated performers. Two in particular that are well worth checking out are Arfe II and Casa Matías.

Arfe II is well established and extremely popular with the locals because it presents impromtu flamenco sessions during the afternoons on Saturdays, Sundays and holidays. This is the type of venue where musicians turn up to participate in a jam-style session, while customers participate with spontaneous outbusrts of dance. This is advisable for the visitor who wants to encounter a little of the Sevillian way of life, because it offers a true demonstration of their love of the fiesta.

Casa Matias has character and plenty of history, as the dusty old bottles and paraphernalia surrounding Seville's devotion to Semana Santa, flamenco, and bullfighting will demonstrate. This tiny bar is also famed for the spontaneous flamenco sessions that take place over on certain afternoons, usually Thursday, Saturday and Monday. However, the arrival of a guitarist is usually enough to incite a spontaneous session any day of the week.

This area also boasts one of Seville's better flamenco tablaos, although, as with the majority, the cost of drinking and eating will be considerably higher than the previously mentioned bars.

El Arenal (C/ Rodo 7) is situated in a 17th century building and claims to offer a pure and genuine flamenco show. This tablao has been entertaining flamenco aficionados for more than 30 years and its popularity was boosted when the New York Times described it as 'the best flamenco in Seville'. The flamenco is entertaining, but the highlight of the show is the *fin de fiesta* (the final act), when all of the performers are encouraged to engage in an outburst of dance, recreating the traditional Gypsy family fiesta.

On one very hot August night in Seville, I decided to give it a try. The venue was not instantly recognisable as a flamenco bar - just a heavy old door which offered no hint of the mysterious beauty it concealed.

On arrival, I was greeted by a doorman, who informed me that it would cost thirty euros to enter. I accepted and was shown to a table. The entrance fee included the first drink. The table was very elegantly decorated with a small glass oil lamp, heavy tablecloth with cutlery and glasses set out like an exclusive restaurant. The waiters, dressed in bow ties and waistcoats informed me that a menu was available, but, thankfully, I had already eaten.

The artistes, three guitarists, a violinist, and a collection of singers and dancers, all performed to a very high standard, although I'm not certain pure and genuine would be the correct description. Nevertheless, it was very entertaining. The show was of better quality than I had come to expect from a tablao.

The only commercial feel was created by hordes Japanese tourists who were snapping away with their cameras throughout the majority of the show.

In Granada, the districts of the Albaicín and Sacromonte are where the majority of the flamenco tablaos are located. Here, one will find the famous caves, which, until 1610, were occupied by the Moors. After the expulsion of the Moors, the Gypsies moved into the cave dwellings. In the early 19th century, the romantic writers began to tell of the Gypsy dancing and singing that took place here. This attracted hordes foreign visitors, as it still does to this day.

In 1908, a cave was transformed into one of the first tablaos, *La Zambra,* and soon, many more followed. The area of Sacromonte is still very famous for its flamenco tablaos.

The quality of the flamenco varies, but the one thing they all have in common is that they are expensive. Some will advertise free entry, then charge around twelve euros for the first drink, and only slightly less for any others one consumes. Others charge somewhere in the region of 25 euros entrance fee, but offer a free glass of sangria, or, at least, something that resembles it.

One tablao which was very entertaining is *Los Tarantos* in Torremolinos, which opened in 1999. Sadly, this establishment has since closed.

The two main dancers, La Trini and El Carrete, were supported by two younger dancers, one of whom is La Trini's daughter, Carmen; the other, her boyfriend, Cristobal.

Carmen and Cristobal were the crowd pleasers, displaying youth and vitality in their dance, which was well rehearsed, although visual and enjoyable. These two dancers were what the tourists come to see, but it was the appearance of El Carrete that really grabbed their attention.

Appearing from the side door, dressed in a black suit, complete with cordovan hat and walking cane, his fingers and arms outstretched, legs straight, head and back almost at right-angle, he takes two or three steps on to the stage and pauses. He begins to move elegantly, but humorously, around the stage. Throwing his hat and cane to one side, he starts with a slow zapateado, which progresses into a frenzied display of this dedicated dancer's ability of the feet.

Throughout his dance, his long fingers are forced through his dark hair, his piercing Gypsy eyes changing to a mischievous smile, as he toys with his audience.

The flamenco world is full of flamboyant Gypsy performers that started their careers in the streets of Andalusia and went on to achieve fame and fortune while performing on some of the most coveted stages in the world. José Losada - El Carrete, is one of these. Born in Antequera, Málaga in 1943, he has dedicated his whole life to performing, teaching and promoting the art of flamenco dance. He is a dazzling showman whose dance routines have delighted audiences in Europe, Asia and America for more than 50 years. He acquired his artistic name, which means spool or reel, from his mother, a dancer called La Carreta, who made a living selling the potent biznaga flowers in the streets of Antequera: his father worked as a donkey shearer.

El Carrete began dancing in the streets when he was four, performing for tossed coins in order to help his family survive. As a child, he would sneak into the local cinema to shelter from the cold, and it was here that he developed his love of the movies and Hollywood. His fascination with dance began after watching Fred Astaire on the golden screen, and this is obvious in his dance routines today. His dance style is erratic to say the least, and he can make the most sombre flamenco styles come alive with his energetic, rattling footwork.

One of his first professional engagements was at the Tablao El Refugio in Málaga, and it was the owner of this establishment that bequest him his first suit and dancing shoes. It was also a place that would become his temporary home, because he was allowed to sleep in the store room, which had, he once told me, the luxury of a paraffin lamp for heat.

He also danced in the Taberna Gitana, and from here he went to the popular Bodegas El Pimpi, where he became part of the flamenco group known as Los Vargas. It was during this period that José would begin a life of shoulder-rubbing with famous stars like Sean Connery, Frank Sinatra and Anthony Quinn.

Malaga was a hive of activity during the 1950s and the city centre would be swarming with tourists, and US servicemen, whose ships would be docked in the port. During the day, José worked as a shoe shiner, although he subsidised his earnings by selling contraband cigarettes, from a concealed compartment of his shoe box.

The young dancer was soon to discover the exciting new flamenco scene that was taking place in a small town just 12 kilometres along the Costa del Sol. Torremolinos was still a fishing town when El Carrete first arrived, but it soon became the most popular town on the coast, and it boasted several flamenco tablaos that catered for the new influx of British and American tourists.

One of his first jobs in Torremolinos was at the infamous *El Mañana Bar*, but it would be in the popular tablao *El Jaleo,* where he would shine like a star amongst the stars.

Camarón de la Isla, who called El Carrete the 'monster', was said to have been mesmerised by his dance, and would often turn up unannounced to perform with him.

In 1977, he moved to Los Angeles, where he worked in a flamenco tablao in Santa Monica, and it was here that he would be captivated by the American Jazz scene.

On returning to Spain, and while working in Madrid, El Carrete turned down a contract that may have been his stepping stone to international stardom. Antonio Gades offered him a part in a film that was to be produced by Carlos Saura. José declined the offer; instead, he borrowed money from Antonio Gades in order to return to Torremolinos to help a cousin who was experiencing difficulties at the time.

During the 1980's, El Carrete appeared in numerous tablaos and hotels along the Costa del Sol, and he eventually opened his own club in Torremolinos in 1990.

Today he still lives in Torremolinos and can be seen on most days strolling through the streets accompanied by his ever-loyal Yorkshire terriers, Gazpachuelo and Gazpachulino.

El Carrete lives for flamenco; it is his lifeline, his inspiration, his reason for living. Everything he does is flamenco, even the way he walks. He is a gentleman, always very respectful, but with a terrible affection for the attention of the females, especially any of the English ones who might be part of our company when we went for a night out at Los Tarantos.

Although most people believe flamenco to be very serious and sombre, and at times it can be, there is a lighter side to it portrayed by the fiesteros. The fiestero, who usually has a gift for telling amusing stories, dances and sings, often inventing the words as they go along. El Carrete possesses all of these qualities.

One of the biggest problems for the tourists and foreigner aficionados is that they will not normally know where to go to witness pure flamenco, because this is something that is not usually advertised on large posters.

To capture that moment of pure spontaneous outburst, when flamenco just happens, with no rehearsals, just instinct and passion - when the dancer or singer explodes into a frenzy of Gypsy mayhem - is quite often a chance experience. The best performances of orthodox flamenco are unplanned and it is a case of simply being in the right place at the right time. No matter how established or authentic the tablaos claim to be, they will never give the adrenalin rush that a spontaneous recital will produce.

Apart from the tablaos, there are the flamenco peñas and these give a more traditional insight into flamenco. These clubs are normally run by aficionados of the art whose main aim is the flamenco, and not to extract as much money as they can from the customers who use them.

Most towns will have at least one flamenco peña, and the major cities will have anything between ten and thirty. The peñas are always very welcoming to outsiders or newcomers, and are wonderful places to find out about up-and-coming flamenco events.

These are a lot more traditional in the style of flamenco that is presented, which will, on most occasions, be cante jondo. These clubs will normally stage a concurso de cante, which is the competition that precedes the town's flamenco festival, and the winner of the local competition will go on to perform in the festival alongside the more established artistes.

It is not only the style and quality of flamenco that stands out from the tablaos, but also the price one will pay for a night out at one of these establishments. There is rarely an entrance fee, and the price of the drinks will be the same as a local bar.

The peñas are normally named after one of the town's most famous artistes, like the Peña Flamenca Antonio Mairena in Mairena del Alcor, which is situated in a restored palace, complete with a small museum and amphitheatre where the local flamenco festival is held.

One of Cádiz's best peñas is the Peña Chano Lobato, situated in Avenida Marconi; and the Peña Flamenca Gaditana Enrique el Mellizo, which can be found on the Paseo de San Felipe.

Jerez de la Frontera has many old peñas, especially in the areas of San Miguel and Santiago, where Fernando Terremoto, Antonio Chacón, and El Sordera all have their names attached to one.

End note

The research for this book has been the most enjoyable 'work' I have ever done. Many hours have been spent at festivals in charming locations on warm summer nights. I've listened to the best flamenco in some of Andalusia's most picturesque settings, and I have become entangled in one of the most mystery-shrouded cultures to emerge from this seductive land. I've had worse jobs.

The main reason behind this book was to inform English-speaking people who might have an interest in flamenco about the superb flamenco that exists in Andalusia. This desire emerged simply because of the problems I encountered when I first became drawn to this wonderful art.

With today's modern technology, flamenco is far more accessible than it was fifty years ago; or one hundred years before that, when singers would have to walk miles to a small village to learn a particular style of song. With today's recording facilities, many of the old shellac records have been digitally re-mastered, so we can now listen to the likes of Antonio Chacón or Manuel Torres and compare them to the next generation of artistes.

But what makes flamenco so contagious or fascinating? Why, more than two hundred years after the first singers were documented, are we still talking about them, especially the likes of Paco la Luz and El Pinini, who never recorded anything?

Flamenco is an art that is passed on from one generation to the next, and what that next generation does with it is the defining question.

There are some artistes that continue to promote the jondo song and dance styles of their ancestors, but they are an elite few that make their names by simply doing something which comes natural to them.

Today, the commercial scene tempts many of the younger generation (as well as some of the more established ones) into performing and recording a modern style of flamenco, which is fused with pop music – new flamenco.

Many of today's artistes that come under the umbrella name of flamenco perform a music that has been far removed from its original structure.

There are those who will argue that it is time we stopped harping on about the 19th and early 20th centuries, and start looking to the future, if flamenco is to have one. The trend in today's flamenco leans more towards pop music, with the addition of electric bass, keyboards, drums and harmonies, all of which go against the tradition of flamenco.

Many of today's artistes experiment with different musical styles on their CDs. Capullo de Jerez's last offering, *Canela y Flor*, has lost all the raw energy for which he is renowned. The songs are more musically arranged using keyboards and piano. Today's artistes don't seem to get the same disapproval that Juanito Valderrama and Pepe Marchena got for doing basically the same thing in the 1950s.

The world that the average Spaniard lives in today differs greatly from the Spain of just fifty years ago, especially in Andalusia. The artistes of old sang to provide for their families and put food on the table. When one considers the average wage for a night's work would have been as little as ten pesetas, compared to the thousands of euros demanded by today's artistes, one can see how dramatically the lifestyles of these artistes has changed. The entrance fee for one of their concerts will cost as much as any other rock or pop concert.

However, there are a few younger artistes who are making their names by concentrating on orthodox flamenco. Miguel Poveda, the young singer from Badalona, is proving to be one of the most promising artistes of today, although he is starting to fuse his flamenco with pop and copla.

One of the most unusual 21st century ways of performing flamenco that I have witnessed was performed by a standup. Unfortunately, I do not recall his name, but he was a comedian who told his jokes to the rhythm of the bulería. The punch line was met with cries of olé!, upon which, the comedian would burst into a short dance routine, before composing himself for the next joke. Was this the future of flamenco? I certainly hope not, although it was rather entertaining.

I believe that cante jondo has a future and it will not just be pushed to one side by the commercial scene once again. Even though flamenco is not as much a part or a way of life as it used to be, there are those who still adhere to this way, and if one is fortunate enough to experience it, they might begin to understand why flamenco is so captivating.

The Gypsy families of Andalusia live in very close-knit communities and their large families are weaned on the style of flamenco from that particular area. Their daily routines are accompanied by flamenco dance and song, whether while cooking or doing the washing, working the fields or offering produce at the market. The children are absorbed in this lifestyle from birth, which explains how they understand, and can perform, flamenco from such a young age.

During the 1970s, many of the large Gypsy communities in areas such as Triana were dismantled and dispersed to the outskirts of the city, and the natural flamenco ambience of the district disappeared with them.

Many of the old *casa de vecinos* (communal dwellings shared by numerous families) were either demolished and replaced by modern apartment blocks, or renovated and turned into trendy dwellings.

Certain areas of Andalusia still have a community way of life and none more so than in places like Jerez de la Frontera, Lebrija, Utrera and Morón de la Frontera: these areas are still producing singers of the traditional styles of flamenco.

I am often accused of being old-fashioned, possibly to some degree of truth, as I prefer the untouched rural side of Andalusia to the tourist-destroyed areas of the Costas. The tranquillity of places like Morón de la Frontera and Utrera is much more appealing to me than the hubbub of the Costa del Sol, and my views about flamenco are very much the same. My preference is the traditional flamenco song and dance, not the commercial fusion style of flamenco that can be found in the glitzy clubs and casinos of the costal resorts.

Some people may start with commercial flamenco and then become interested in the history of this culture, and, perhaps the jondo style of flamenco. But be warned, because once the cante jondo has become an acquired taste, it is most often the case that one will only want to listen to the old tongue that sings it.

The Gypsies have played a great part in the evolution and the preservation of flamenco, and it is with them that the art of flamenco is at its best. Whether one believes that flamenco is the music of the Gypsies, or that it is, as García Lorca described it, 'the greatest creation of the Spanish people', will continue to be debated for centuries to come.

One thing that is certain is that if it were not for the Gypsy communities of Andalusia, flamenco would probably have dissolved into the abyss of time. There have been many non-Gypsy artistes of great esteem, from the earliest days of the eighteenth century right up until present day, but compared to the amount of Gypsy masters, this number is low.

Whether the Gypsies were the first performers of flamenco or not, it does seem that it is with them that the art comes into its own. I am not suggesting that the Gypsies invented all styles of flamenco. I am merely saying that in my opinion it is more theirs than anyone else's, as they have melded and adapted non-Gypsy styles, like the fandangos, into their own personal creation.

I do not profess to be an expert on the art of flamenco, just a passionate follower of it, and I have merely offered my personal opinions and preferences throughout this book.

Other aficionados must seek out the styles and artistes they prefer, because like all art, everyone sees something different.

Flamenco is not just a strange form of music, which to the unfamiliar sounds like the painful tones of a desolate race; it is a magical gift that has been bestowed upon the people of Andalusia. It is a contagious dance that is so passionate it will leave one spellbound, or an outburst of duende-fuelled song that invades the soul, or a light-hearted bit of fun where nothing seems to matter and time is unimportant.

Long may it continue!

Directory

This section is a directory of the peñas and tablaos that can be found throughout Andalusia. It does not, however, list all of these establishments, only some of the better ones that can be found in the places discussed throughout this book.

Andalusia has hundreds of flamenco tablaos, some offering a lot better quality of flamenco than others. Unfortunately, they are normally expensive places, but it must be remembered that most have at least two or three dancers, plus a singer and guitarist, who, along with the other overheads of the club, need paying. The types of tablao vary considerably, from the price of the drinks, to whether there is an entrance fee, and, from my experiences, the quality or originality of the flamenco. My only advice is to steer clear of the tacky-type clubs advertised in the lobbies of hotels. They will often proclaim to offer the most 'pure Andalusian-Gypsy culture', a free glass of sangría on entry, and the chance to take home a souvenir photograph of yourself wearing a plastic cordovan hat.

Unfortunately, there are plenty of these types of clubs, and their aim seems to be to extract as much money out of the unsuspecting tourist as is possible.

Most of the tablaos will be open in the afternoon so that tickets can be reserved in advance, and it may be wise to check out the bar tariff before committing oneself.

I have also listed some of the major flamenco festivals, as to visit one of these is an absolute must for the hardened aficionado, and a good introduction for the novice. Whether this is the Bienal in Seville, which has been running for nearly thirty years, or one of the smaller one-night festivals in somewhere like Utrera or Ronda, it should be a most wonderful experience. They will, with the odd exception, be staged between the months of May and September.

Tablaos

Cádiz

Taberna Flamenca La Cava
Antonio López 16.
CP11004
www.flamencolacava.com

Granada

Cueva de la Faraona
Camino de Sacromonte
CP18010

Cueva del Roció
Camino de Sacromonte
CP 18010

Los Tarantos
Camino de Sacromonte
CP 18010
Tel 958 22 45 25

Zambra, María la Canastera.
Camino de Sacromonte
CP 18010
Tel 958 12 11 83

Zambra Gitana, Venta El Gallo
Barranco de los negros, 5
Sacromonte
CP18010
Tel 958 22 05 91
www.ventaelgallo.com

Jerez de la Frontera

El Lagá del Tio Parrilla
Plaza Becerra 5
CP 11408
Tel 956 33 83 34

La Taberna Flamenca
Angostillo de Santiago S/n
CP 11408
Tel 649 38 39 78

Málaga

El Tablao
C/Arenal 1
Tel. 952 06 12 55

Seville

El Arenal
Rodo 7
CP 41001
Tel 954 21 64 92

El Patio Sevillano
Paseo Colon, 11-A
CP 41001

Los Gallos
Plaza de Santa Cruz, 11
CP 41004

Anselma
C/ Pagés del Corro 49 (Triana)
Puerta de Triana, Castilla 137
CP 41010
Tel 954 37 25 02

Peñas

Arahal

Peña Pastora Pavón
La Niña de los Peines, Pacho S/n
CP 416000
Tel 955 84 03 30

Cádiz

Peña Flamenca Chano Lobato
Avda Marconi 2
CP 11009
Tel 956 26 14 15

Peña Flamenca Gaditana Enrique el Mellizo
Paseo de San Felipe S/n
CP 11004
Tel 956 22 19 85

Dos Hermanas

Peña Cultural Flamenca Juan Talega
Carlos 1 de España 39
CP 41700
Tel 954 72 22 19

Granada

Federación Provincial de Peñas Flamencas Granadinas
La Solana 23
CP 18198
Tel 958 50 21 86

Peña Flamenca La Platería
Placeta de Toqueros 7
CP18010
Tel 958 22 77 12

Jerez de la Frontera

Centro Cultural Flamenco
Don Antonio Chacón, Salas 2
CP 11403
Tel 956 34 74 72

Asociación Cultural Flamenca
Fernando Terremoto, Terremoto de Jerez S/n.
Tel 956 34 49 01

Lebrija

Peña Flamenca Pepe Montaraz
Callejón de los Frailes 6,
CP 41740
Tel 955 97 12 72

Mairena del Alcor

Casa del Arte Flamenco
Antonio Mairena, Plz A. Mairena, 14
CP 41510
Tel 955 94 27 94

Málaga

Peña Flamenca Fosforito
Arenisca 12, Santa Cristina
CP 29006
Tel 952 35 11 15

Peña Flamenca Juan Breva
C/ Beatas, Plz La Merced
Tel 952 21 08 76

Peña Flamenca El Piyayo. Urb las Pedrizas 2. CP 29730.
Rincón de la Victoria. Tel 952 40 48 29

Morón de la Frontera

Peña Flamenca Montegil
Arahal 40
CP 41530
Tel 954 85 08 21

Seville

Federación Provincial de Sevilla D Entidades Flamencas
Dante 1, Aula 26
CP41006
Tel 954 64 19 76
*There are in excess of 50 peñas in the province of Seville, so I have only included this federation, where information of all the clubs can be obtained.

Peña Curro de Utrera
Porche de Santa María 5
CP 41710
Tel 954 86 20 37

Festivals

Alhaurin de la Torre.	Festival Torre del Cante. June.
Alora.	Festival de cante grande. July.
Antequera.	Noche Flamenca de Santa María. Aug.
Dos Hermanas.	Festival de Flamenco Juan Talega. June.
Granada	Noche Flamenca de Albaicin. Aug.
Jerez de la Frontera.	Festival de Jerez. April.
Lebrija.	Caracolá Lebrijana. July.
Málaga.	Bienal- Málaga en Flamenco. Sept.
Mairena del Alcor.	Festival de Cante Jondo A.Mairena. Sept.
Morón de la Frontera.	Gazpacho Andaluz. Aug.
Ronda.	Festival de Cante Grande. Aug.
Seville.	Bienal de Arte Flamenco. Sept.
	bienal@bienal-flamenco.org
	Tel 954 59 28 72.
Torremolinos.	Festival Flamenco. Aug.
Utrera.	Potaje Gitano. June.

Glossary

Abandalao. Song style in the rhythm of the *fandango*, originating in the Serranía de Ronda.

A Golpe. The purest form of flamenco. Without guitar accompaniment; sung to the rhythm of a stick or knuckles on a tabletop.

Alboreá. Gypsy wedding song.

Alegría. Lively song style originating in Cádiz.

A Palo Seco. Pure flamenco song style without the accompaniment of the guitar.

Apodo. Nickname or stage name.

Bailaor/a. Male/female flamenco dancer, as opposed to all other dancers - *bailarín/a*

Baile. Flamenco dance, as opposed to danza, which refers to all other styles of dance.

Baile de Mantón. Dance performed by the female with the use of a shawl.

Baji.* Luck.

Bambera. Folkloric song style.

Bandolas. A form of *fandango* from the mountain areas of Málaga: its lyrics normally refer to banditry.

Barrio. District or neighbourhood.

Bata de cola. Flamenco dress with a long flowing train.

*Bengue.** Evil spirit/ devil.

Buena Ventura. Fortune telling.

Braceo. Arm work of the dancer.

Bulería. Song style that occupies a supreme position in the world of flamenco because it is its most flexible and wide open to spontaneity.

Bulería por soleá. A cross between bulería and soleá, but with a slower rhythm, like that of the soleá.

Café cantantes. Flamenco bars and cafes that sprung up during the golden age of flamenco, similar to modern-day tablao*s*.

Calo/Cali. Name by which the Gypsies refer to themselves and their language.

Calle. Street

Camelar. * To love.

Caña. Song style from the soleá family, which is thought to have originated in Ronda.

Cantaor/a. Flamenco singer as opposed to cantante, which is applied to all other singers.

Cante chico. Lighter style of flamenco song like the *tangos*, and *alegrías*.

Cantes de ida y vuelta. Flamenco-influenced songs from Latin America.

Cante Gitano. Gypsy song.

Cante Grande. The heavy, or deep song, like the *deblas* and *martinetes*.

Cante Jondo. The deep song, flamenco at its purest.

Cante de Levante. Songs of the east.

Cante pa Alante. This refers to when the singer is seated.

Cante pa Atrás. This is when the singer stands behind the dancer.

Cantiñas. Family of song styles that includes the *alegría*.

Caracol. Means snail. A song style that originates from Cádiz.

Carceleras. Prisons songs. A style similar to the *martinete*, except for the lyrics, which are normally about prison life.

Cartegenera. A fandango from Almería.

Castañuelas. Castanets.

Caseta. Small marquee or hut- type bars erected for feria*s*.

Chorizo. Spanish sausage spiced with paprika.

Chungo.* Bad or ugly.

Churros. Deep-fried dough rings, often eaten with hot drinking chocolate.

Compás. Roughly translated, it means rhythm or beat. If you have good *compás*, it means you have natural rhythm.

Copla. A verse that can be sung.

Cuadro. Group; cuadro flamenco, flamenco group.

Debla. One of the oldest song forms from the *toña* family, which is sung unaccompanied. The word debla means goddess in Cali.

Duende. Possession, a state of mind. *'All that has black sounds has duende.'*

Falseta. A small run or fill-in on the guitar - the twiddly bits the guitarist plays during the singer's pauses.

Fandango. Flamenco style which originated around Málaga. Found in various forms in every province of Andalusia.

Farruca. A style of dance from northern Spain.

Feria. Fair.

Fiesta. Party or celebration.

Fiestero. An all-round performer who sings, dances and tells amusing stories.

Fino. Sherry from Jerez de la Frontera.

Flamencologist. Someone who studies the history and origins of flamenco.

Gacho Non-Gypsy.

Gaditano/a. A native of Cádiz.

Gazpacho. A cold Andalusian soup made from tomatoes, cucumber, water, vinegar and bread.

Gitano/a. Gypsy. The word gitano refers to the Gypsies of Southern France and Spain, but it is used to describe Gypsies in general.

Golpe. To strike or hit.

Gracia. Wit or charm. When referring to the dance it means grace.

Gracioso. Amusing, funny.

Granadino. A person from Granada.

Granaina. A fandango from Granada, although some attribute its creation to Don Antonio *Chacón*.

Guajira. Style of ida y vuelta.

Guiri. Tourist or foreigner. (normally used in a derogatory way)

¡Hijo de puta! Son of a bitch!

Jabera. A form of Fandango from Málaga, which is free of rhythm.

Jaleo. Hellraising. The encouragement of the artiste by the audience and the other performers.

Jerezano. A person from Jerez de la Frontera.

Jondo. Deep.

Juerga. Flamenco jam session/party.

Juncal.* Graceful.

Lachi.* Shy.

Letras. Words (of a song).

Liviana. Song style of the *siguiriya* family.

Madre. Mother; often pronounced without the 'd'.

Malagueña. Local *fandango* from Málaga.

Malagueño/a. A person from Málaga

Martinete. Song style born in the blacksmiths` forges of Triana.

Mataora. Tester of a bride's virginity.

Minera. Song style from eastern Andalusia.

Moros. Muslims.

Nazareno. Hooded penitents.

Palmas. Clapping.

Palmero. Person who keeps rhythm by clapping.

Palo. Style (palo seco – dry style)

Panda. Group who perform the verdiales.

Pasos. Religious images carried through the streets of Seville during Semana Santa.

Payo. Non-gypsy

Peña. Bar/club.

Pesetas. Old Spanish currency.

Petenera. Song style believed to have originated in Paterna del Rio.

Pitos. Finger clicking.

Polo. Song style from Ronda, related to the *caña*.

¡Por Dios! For God's sake! / For the love of God.

Puchero. Hearty stew made with various meats, *chorizo, tocino, morcilla*, chickpeas, vegetables and potatoes.

Pueblo. Village: also means the people.

Puro. Pure.

Rachi.* Night.

Rasgueado. A rhythm effect created by striking the muted guitar strings.

Romeria. Pilgrimage.

Rondeña. A very old *fandango abandolao* from Ronda.

Rumba. Song style from Cuba.

Saeta. Ardent songs sung to the images of the Passion during Semana Santa

Semana Santa. Easter, Holy Week.

Señorito. Wealthy gentleman.

Sevillanas. A popular dance, obligatory during feria week in Seville, and every other feria in Andalucia

Siguiriya. Gypsy flamenco song that is considered the heart of flamenco.

Soleá. Another of the pure flamenco styles that originated around Seville, some of the best coming from Triana, Utrera and Alcalá de Guadaira.

Sonidos Negros. Black sounds.

Tablao. Flamenco nightclub, or the stage where dancer performs.

Tango. Lively Gypsy flamenco style.

Tanguillos. Festive flamenco songs that originate from Cádiz.

Tapa. Savoury snacks. It was once customary to give a free tapa with each drink purchased; a custom that is little practised today.

Taranta. Song form from Almería.

Tiento. Song style from the tango family but with a slower rhythm.

Tinaja A ceramic percussion instrument.

Toña. Believed to be the root of all styles of flamenco, dating back to at least 1770 in Jerez de la Frontera.

Traje Gitana. Gypsy dress worn at the feria and by flamenco dancers.

Triana. District of Seville where many forms of *cante* are thought to have originated.

Trono. Floats that are carried through the streets of Málaga during Semana Santa.

Verdiales. Folk songs from the mountain areas that surround Málaga.

Voz Afillá. A rough, gravelly voice.

Zambra. Song style performed at a Gypsy wedding: also style of dance from the Sacromonte area of Granada.

Zapateado. The intricate foot work performed by the dancer.

Zorongo. A black American dance, converted by the Gypsies to a flamenco style in the early 20th century.

The words marked with * are Gypsy, or Caló, words.

Discography

It would be near impossible to recommend a list of music or singers, for, like wine, everyone has a different palate. A list of personal favourites would be easier, but that would not be of much use to anyone else.

When I first started to buy flamenco CDs, I normally bought what other people had recommended or, in some cases, I brought compilation CDs. Compilations are a good way to find out about certain singers or guitarists. There is one collection published by EMI, with each disc dedicated to one style. It's a good idea to invest one's money in one of these, because it will give one the opportunity to decide which artists they prefer. It's a bit like eating tapas, better to sample a small offering of several dishes, than to go for a dish that might not be to your liking.

My best advice is to look in the bargain bins often located outside of tourist gift shops, because one can occasionally pick up CDs by Tomás Pavon, Manuel Torre or Don Antonio Chacón.

Also, look for the old singers, like El Chocolate, who excels in the siguiriyas and tarantos; Agujetas, a master of the martinete and palos secos; and artistes from Utrera like El Perrate, Gaspar de Utrera and La Fernanda for soleares.

Any artiste from Jerez de la Frontera would be a wise choice, especially La Paquera or Terremoto de Jerez for bulerías. Other Jerezano singers to look out for are the old masters like Tio El Borrico, La Piriñaca and El Sordera, some of the most orthodox voices in the history of flamenco.

Much the same applies to singers from Lebrija, in particular, Miguel el Funi, Inés Bacán and Maria La Perrata.

For the fandangos, Don Antonio Chacón was one of the masters, as was Juan Breva, while Enrique Morente also excelled in fandangos, granaínas, cartageneras and malagueñas.

Of the younger generation of flamencos, José Mercé is, in my opinion, one of the best overall singers, but he is also an artist who performs and records much flamenco pop. Search out his earlier recordings, pre-2000, as these I would recommend for any serious aficionado's collection.

Miguel Poveda is one of the most talented young flamenco singers around at the moment, and, although he is not Gypsy, and has no artistic predecessors in his family, he has become something of a revelation.

Pitingo is another fine singer who is capable of performing fine orthodox cante, especially the Soleares de La Fernanda de Utrera. Born in Huelva, this young cantaor has been weaned on flamenco: his great grandmother was the cousin of Pastora and Tomás Pavon, yet he too fuses flamenco with soul and gospel music, a style he calls *soulerías.*

I could go on, but it will be up to the individual's personal taste, and like a fine old Cognac, it this mature with time.

The guitarists are also many, but any of the 'old school' like Niño Ricardo, Sabicas, Diego del Gastor or Melchor de Marchena, would be the best introduction, both for fans of the solo instrument, and the accompanist.

The last guitarist will need little introduction, even probably to those unfamiliar with flamenco. Paco de Lucia's days as the accompanist of

Camarón de la Isla produced some of the best orthodox flamenco ever recorded.

CDs

Antonio Mairena / Enrique de Melchor and Pedro Peña.
El Calor de Mis Recuerdos. Pasarela.

Bernarda de Utrera/ Pedro Peña and Antonio Moya. **A Fernanda**.
Universal Music Spain.

Camarón de la Isla /Paco de Lucía and Tomatito. **Calle Real**.
Polygram Ibérica

Camarón de la Isla /Tomatito. **Paris 1987.** (live) Universal music.

Capullode Jerez/Niño Jero and Diego Amaya. **Este soy yo.**

Chano Lobato/ Paco del Gastor. **Aroma.** Pasarela, S.L

Curro de Utrera/José Antonio Rodríguez. **El Cante De**… Dial discs.

Diego del Gastor. **El Eco de unos Toques.** El Flamenco Vive.

Enrique Morente/Sabicas. **Morente/ Sabicas.** BMG Music Spain.

Fernanda y Bernarda de Utrera / Manolo Domínguez. **Raza y Compás**.
Pasarela.

Inés Bacán / Antonio Moya and Pedro Mª Peña. **Pasión**. Universal.

José Mercé/ Enrique de Melchor and Luis Habichuela. **Cuerpo y Alma.**
Fono music

José Mercé/ Vicente Amigo. **Del Amanecer**. Virgin. (Yerbabuena)

Moraito. **Morao Morao**. Nuevos Medios.

Tomás de Perrate y Familia/ Antonio Moya **Utrera Flamenca**.
Fonographic del Sur.

COMPILATIONS

El Cante Flamenco. 3CDs (Fosforito, El Lebrijano, Terremoto, etc.)
Universal Music Spain.
Nuestro Flamenco Colección 1 RTVE Música.
Antonio Mairena-Terremoto de Jerez-Melchor de Marchena.
Nuestro Flamenco Colección 2 RTVE Música.

DVDs

*Rito y Geografía del Cante. Alba Editories.RTVE.
*Flamencos en los archivos de RTVE. Alba Editories
*Puro y Jondo. (14 DVDs) Divisa Ediciones. TVE.
* *These are Collections of DVDs that can be purchased as a series or individually.*

Printed in Great Britain
by Amazon

37019010R00136